Spanish for the Green Industry

Jennifer Thomas

Upper Saddle River, New Jersey 07458

Library of Congress Cataloging-in-Publication Data

Thomas, Jennifer.
  Spanish for the green industry / Jennifer Thomas.
    p. cm.
  English and Spanish.
  ISBN 0-13-048041-X
    1. Spanish language—Conversation and phrase books (for landscaping industry
employees) I. Title.

PC4120.L35 T56 2001
468.3'421'02471—dc21   2001058089

Editor-in-Chief: Steve Helba
Executive Acquisitions Editor: Debbie Yarnell
Associate Editor: Kimberly Yehle
Editorial Assistant: Sam Goffinet
Managing Editor: Mary Carnis
Production Management: Carlisle Communications, Ltd.
Production Editor: Bridget Lulay
Director of Manufacturing and Production: Bruce Johnson
Manufacturing Buyer: Cathleen Petersen
Marketing Manager: Jimmy Stephens
Creative Director: Cheryl Asherman
Senior Design Coordinator: Miguel Ortiz
Cover Design: Amy Rosen
Cover Illustration: Golf course, courtesy of Tony Stone Images;
Man shoveling, courtesy of PhotoDisc, Inc.; Landscaper in dust
mask and goggles, courtesy of PhotoEdit, Tony Freeman;
flower garden, courtesy of PhotoDisc, Inc.

Pearson Education LTD.
Pearson Education Australia PTY, Limited
Pearson Education Singapore, Pte. Ltd.
Pearson Education North Asia, Ltd.
Pearson Education Canada, Ltd.
Pearson Educación de Mexico, S.A. de C.V.
Pearson Education—Japan
Pearson Education Malaysia, Pte. Ltd.

Prentice Hall

10 9 8 7 6 5 4 3 2
ISBN 0-13-048041-X

CONTENTS

PREFACE

PURPOSE

The Spanish and English for the Green Industry training materials have been developed specifically for those who would like to work more productively and effectively with their diverse co-workers. The purpose of this course is to prepare you for that challenge. This training program will provide you with the necessary skills needed to be successful working in an organization with a diverse staff. You will learn:

- Industry specific vocabulary
- How to assign tasks, follow up, correct and praise behavior
- Key cultural differences
- Team building tips

Since United States' service industries hire many Spanish–speaking employees, bilingual and bicultural employees are very needed and welcomed. The skills you learn in this training program will prove to be very practical and marketable for many years to come.

Benefits of Studying *Spanish* and *English for the Green Industry*

- Improves front line supervisors' ability to communicate
- Increases productivity
- Improves safety
- Increases employee retention and referrals
- Builds teamwork, motivation, and rapport
- Improves cultural leadership skills of front line supervisors
- Increases confidence and comfort level working in a diverse setting
- Provides convenience and availability since it is an on-site class
- Provides consistency between University study and company training
- Oral proficiency in Spanish and English is a valuable skill to add to one's resume

SUPPORT MATERIALS

For the Student

The textbook includes Spanish and English word lists and corresponding pictures, interactive role play exercises, crossword puzzles, dialogues, review activities, and a Spanish/English dictionary. Each chapter contains a cultural reading as well as several team-building tips. A set of flashcards also allows students to review and practice the vocabulary together.

The audiocassette tape provides the correct pronunciation of the vocabulary, and it serves as a follow up oral quiz.

For the Facilitator

The Facilitator's Guide offers many suggestions, teaching methods and instructions on how to implement the basic training program. It explains how to facilitate the learning activities and exciting games.

- **Overhead Transparencies** are provided to enhance the facilitator's presentation of the training program. They are popular games that help the participants review the material in an enjoyable atmosphere.

- **Flash Cards** are provided in two sizes. The large set is provided for the facilitator to introduce the vocabulary and to use with the review activities. The small sets allow the students to review and practice with one another in small groups.

- **Tests, Quizzes and Answer Keys** are provided for every chapter and activity in the textbook.

ACKNOWLEDGMENTS

A sincere thanks to Jacky and Jack Thomas, my parents, who introduced me to the game of golf as well as to the Spanish language. The combination of the two led to this training program. I love you.

A special thanks to my hardworking editor, Debbie Yarnell, for recognizing the need for this training program and for believing in me.

Thanks also to TransXpert, Inc. at *www.transXpert.com* for their precise translations; Rob May at *www.dvpolymedia.com* for his many excellent computer skills; Chris Haserot, my illustrator; Joe Drago, my business consultant; and Larry Hickey and his spiritual advice.

Jennifer Thomas
October, 2001

ABOUT SPANISH TRAINING SERVICES

OUR STORY

Spanish Training Services is the leading provider of Green Industry language and cultural training. The company has been written about in *Pro Magazine, Landscape Management, Nursery Management and Production, Grounds Maintenance,* and *Golfdome.*

Spanish Training Services is committed to offering quality language and cultural training to organizations in order to improve the skills of front line managers and employees. The company specializes in training English and Spanish-speaking employees to communicate more effectively and work together more productively.

While other companies and educational organizations are available for learning the Spanish and English language, their material is too broad and Green Industry cross cultural management issues and are not discussed. Spanish Training Services' unique training focus concentrates and is organized around the specific vocabulary and leadership issues needed to carry out one's daily work responsibilities.

Spanish Training Services was founded in 1996 under the vision that the hardworking Latino labor force will continue to rise and that communication and effective leadership skills will play an increasingly important role in the relationships between the United States supervisor, the Hispanic/Latino employee, as well as the company's clients. Spanish Training Services is a privately owned company, headquartered in Evanston, Illinois.

About the Author

Jennifer Thomas first noticed the need for Green Industry managers to learn Spanish when she was playing golf and speaking Spanish with a Latino employee at a golf club near Chicago. The employee lamented, " *¡Rápido!*' That's the only Spanish word my boss knows! That's all he ever says!" They discussed how not knowing one another's language caused them to lose ten to fifteen minutes an hour in productivity trying to explain a task using just body language. The lack of communication had caused misunderstandings, mistakes, and rework.

Shortly after, Ms. Thomas developed and wrote *Spanish for the Green Industry* and *English for the Green Industry*. She is a regular presenter at Green Industry educational conferences, businesses and University Extension offices.

Her unique training methods and customized courses stem from her extensive educational background and experiences living and working in Mexico, Spain, and South America as well as teaching high school Spanish for many years. Ms. Thomas holds a Master's degree in International Management from the American Graduate School for International Management.

As a former tennis teaching professional and junior golf instructor, Ms. Thomas has much experience training, coaching, and motivating all walks of life. She lives in Evanston, Illinois and spends her summers in Green Lake, Wisconsin.

SPANISH PRONUNCIATION

VOWELS

The Spanish *a* is pronounced similar to the English *a* in the word f*a*ther.

father
casa
planta
mala
Ana
mañana

The Spanish *e* is pronounced like the English *e* in the word th*ey*.

they
tres
cerveza
bebe
trece

The Spanish *i* is pronounced like the English *ee* in the word s*ee*.

see
mi
iba
mis
ir
sí

The Spanish *o* is similar to the English *o* in the word n*o* but a much faster, clipped sound.

no
ocho
poco
dos
como
toco

The Spanish *u* is similar to the English *ue* sound in the name S*ue*.

Sue

uno

tu

un

su

universidad

CONSONANTS

The Spanish *q* sounds similar to the English *k*, and is often followed by the letter u.

queso

quinto

quema

que

quiso

The Spanish *j*, and *g* before e or i, sounds similar to the English *h* in the word *happy*.

happy

Jesus

Juan

general

jarra

gente

The Spanish *b* and the *v* have no difference in sound. They sound similar to the English *b* in the word o*bey*.

obey

Alberto

vete

bote

viaje

víctima

The *y* and the *ll* are similar to the English *y* in the word *yard*.

yard

yo

llama

yarda

llover

lluvia

The letter *h* is silent in Spanish.

> hola
> hojas
> hora
> hoy
> hermano

The Spanish *ch* is pronounced like the English *ch* in the word *ch*ild.

> child
> chico
> muchacho
> chile
> coche

The Spanish *ñ* has a sound similar to the English *ny* in the word ca*ny*on.

> canyon
> señor
> mañana
> muñeca
> señorita
> año

The Spanish *r* in an initial position and *rr* in the middle of a word are pronounced with a strong trill.

> Roberto
> perro
> rubio
> rosa
> carro

The Spanish *r* is pronounced like the English *t* in the word gu*tt*er.

> gutter
> para
> arena
> pero

Greetings

PART I   GREETINGS

Good morning.	**Buenos días.**
Good afternoon.	**Buenas tardes.**
Good night.	**Buenas noches.**
Welcome.	**Bienvenidos.**
Hi/Hello	**Hola.**
How's it going?	**¿Qué tal?**
How are you?	**¿Cómo estás?**
Fine, and you?	**Bien. ¿Y tú?**
How's your family?	**¿Cómo está tu familia?**
What's your name?	**¿Cómo te llamas?**
My name is . . .	**Me llamo . . .**
See you later.	**Hasta luego.**
See you tomorrow.	**Hasta mañana.**
Goodbye.	**Adiós.**
Please.	**Por favor.**
Thank you.	**Gracias.**
I'm studying Spanish.	**Estudio español.**
I speak Spanish a little.	**Hablo español un poco.**
Do you speak English?	**¿Hablas inglés?**
Do you understand English?	**¿Comprendes inglés?**

MATCHING EXERCISE

Write the letter of the Spanish phrase next to the English phrase it matches on the left.

1. _____ My name is . . .   a. ¿Cómo estás?

2. _____ How's it going?   b. ¿Qué tal?

3. _____ Fine, and you?   c. Me llamo . . .

4. _____ How's your family?   d. Bien. ¿Y tú?

5. _____ See you tomorrow.   e. Gracias.

6. _____ Hi/Hello.   f. Hasta luego.

7. _____ See you later.   g. Hola.

8. _____ Welcome.   h. Buenos días.

9. _____ Please.   i. ¿Cómo está tu familia?

10. _____ Good morning.   j. Adiós.

11. _____ How are you?   k. Bienvenidos.

12. _____ Thank you.   l. Por favor.

13. _____ Goodbye.   m. Hasta mañana.

CROSSWORD PUZZLES

Across

2. Do you speak English?
5. Good afternoon.
7. Hi/Hello.
8. How are you?
10. Please.
11. How's it going?

Down

1. Good night.
3. Good morning.
4. See you later.
6. Thank you.
9. Goodbye.

Across

1. Estudio español.
6. Buenas tardes.
7. ¿Cómo estás?
8. ¿Qué tal?
9. Hola.
11. Hasta luego.
13. Por favor.
14. ¿Cómo está tu familia?

Down

2. ¿Hablas español?
3. Buenos días.
4. Buenas noches.
5. Adiós.
10. Bienvenidos.
12. Gracias.

TRANSLATION EXERCISE

Translate the following to English:

1. Por favor. _____
2. Gracias. _____
3. Bienvenidos. _____
4. ¿Qué tal? _____
5. Hasta luego. _____
6. Hasta mañana. _____
7. ¿Cómo estás? _____
8. Bien. ¿Y tú? _____
9. Buenos días. _____
10. ¿Cómo está tu familia? _____
_____

Translate the following to Spanish:

1. Good morning. _____
2. How are you? _____
3. How's it going? _____
4. Fine, thanks. And you? _____
_____
5. Good afternoon. _____
6. See you later. _____
7. Welcome. _____
8. How's your family? _____
9. Please. _____
10. Thank you. _____

MULTIPLE CHOICE

Circle the letter of the correct answer.

1. **Please.**
   a. Gracias.
   b. Buenos días.
   c. Adiós.
   d. Por favor.

2. **Thank you.**
   a. Gracias.
   b. Por favor.
   c. Bien.
   d. Hasta luego.

3. **See you tomorrow.**
   a. Buenos días.
   b. Hasta mañana.
   c. Adiós.
   d. Hasta luego.

4. **How are you?**
   a. ¿Qué tal?
   b. ¿Y tú?
   c. Bien, gracias.
   d. ¿Cómo estás?

5. **How's it going?**
   a. Bien. ¿Y tú?
   b. ¿Qué tal?
   c. ¿Cómo estás?
   d. Hasta luego.

6. **See you later.**
   a. Adiós.
   b. Hasta luego.
   c. Hasta mañana.
   d. Buenas noches.

7. **Hello.**
   a. Buenos días.
   b. Hasta luego.
   c. Hola.
   d. Adiós.

8. **Welcome.**
   a. Buenos días.
   b. Adiós.
   c. Bienvenidos
   d. Buenas tardes.

ROLE PLAY

A. **Good morning!** Pretend that you are at a party. In groups of four or five take turns greeting one another. The first student greets the person to the right and then that person greets to the right. Go around the circle two or three times using different phrases such as Hola, Buenos días, Bienvenidos, ¿Qué tal?, etc.

B. **Do you speak English?** Using the directions given in part A ask and answer about your language abilities. Also practice using goodbye phrases with one another.

PART II INTRODUCTIONS

I'm ...	Soy ...
Argentinean	**argentino (a)**
Bolivian	**boliviano (a)**
Chilean	**chileno (a)**
Costa Rican	**costarricense**
Cuban	**cubano (a)**
Dominican	**dominicano (a)**
Ecuadorian	**ecuatoriano (a)**
Guatemalan	**guatemalteco (a)**
Honduran	**hondureño (a)**
Mexican	**mexicano (a)**
Nicaraguan	**nicaragüense**
Panamanian	**panameño (a)**
Paraguayan	**paraguayo (a)**
Peruvian	**peruano (a)**
Puerto Rican	**puertorriqueño (a)**
Salvadorian	**salvadoreño (a)**
United States	**estadounidense**
Uruguayan	**uruguayo (a)**
Venezuelan	**venezolano (a)**

WHERE ARE YOU FROM?

What's your name?	**¿Cómo te llamas?**
My name is Javier.	**Me llamo Javier.**
I'd like to introduce you to ...	**Quiero presentarte a ...**
Nice to meet you.	**Mucho gusto.**
Same to you.	**Igualmente.**
Where are you from?	**¿De dónde eres?**
I'm (from) ...	**Soy (de) ...**
Where is Carlos from?	**¿De dónde es Carlos?**
Carlos is (from) ...	**Carlos es (de) ...**

TEAM BUILDING TIP

Your employees are excited about their new job at your company. They have told their friends and family about it. Make their first week special by posting a big sign for them: "Welcome Carlos Martinez, Pete Black, and Kathy Smith!" If you have a group of employees traveling to your company on a two-day bus ride from the Mexican border, have a delicious welcome dinner for them upon arrival. Music and decorations are always appreciated. Think about when you go to a state educational conference—you're handed a bag of goodies—i.e., t-shirts or baseball caps, notebooks, etc. It's the little things that make an impression.

MATCHING EXERCISE

1. _____ My name is
2. _____ I'm from
3. _____ Carlos is from
4. _____ Nice to meet you
5. _____ From where is
6. _____ What's your name?
7. _____ I'd like to introduce you to
8. _____ Same to you
9. _____ Where are you from?
10. _____ Hello

a. ¿Cómo te llamas?
b. Quiero presentarte a
c. Mucho gusto
d. Soy de
e. Me llamo
f. Igualmente
g. ¿De dónde es?
h. Carlos es de
i. Hola
j. ¿De dónde eres?

CROSSWORD PUZZLES

Across

1. Same to you.
3. What's your name?
8. I'd like to introduce you to . . .

Down

2. Nice to meet you.
4. My name is.
5. I'm from.
6. Where are you from?
7. From where is?

Across

3. ¿Cómo te llamas?
8. ¿De dónde eres?

Down

1. Soy de
2. ¿De dónde es?
4. Igualmente.
5. Mucho gusto.
6. Me llamo
7. Carlos es de

TRANSLATION EXERCISE

Translate the following to English:

1. Carlos es de _____

2. Soy de _____

3. Mucho gusto _____

4. Igualmente _____

5. ¿Cómo te llamas? _____

6. Hola _____

7. Quiero presentarte a _____

8. ¿De dónde eres? _____

9. ¿De dónde es Carlos? _____

10. Me llamo Javier. _____

Translate the following to Spanish:

1. Where are you from? _____

2. Where is Maria from? _____

3. I'm from _____

4. Ana is from _____

5. Hello _____

6. My name is Tomás _____

7. I'd like to introduce you to _____

8. What's your name? _____

9. Pleased to meet you. _____

10. Same to you _____

MULTIPLE CHOICE

Circle the correct answer.

1. **Where are you from?**
   a. Mucho gusto
   b. ¿Cómo te llamas?
   c. ¿De dónde eres?
   d. ¿De dónde es?

2. **My name is**
   a. Soy de
   b. Me llamo
   c. ¿De dónde es?
   d. Mucho gusto

3. **Nice to meet you.**
   a. Igualmente.
   b. Me llamo.
   c. Soy de.
   d. Mucho gusto.

4. **I'm from**
   a. Soy de
   b. Carlos es de
   c. ¿De dónde es?
   d. ¿De dónde eres?

5. **Same to you**
   a. Me llamo
   b. Quiero presentarte a
   c. Igualmente
   d. Mucho gusto

6. **From where is?**
   a. ¿De dónde eres?
   b. ¿De dónde es?
   c. ¿Cómo te llamas?
   d. Soy de

7. **I'd like to introduce you to**
   a. Igualmente
   b. Hola
   c. Mucho gusto
   d. Quiero presentarte a

8. **What's your name?**
   a. ¿Cómo te llamas?
   b. Me llamo
   c. Mucho gusto
   d. Quiero presentarte a

ROLE PLAY

A. Work with a partner. Ask and answer: What's your name? My name is . . . etc. Follow the model.

(Pedro)

ESTUDIANTE A	¿Cómo te llamas?
ESTUDIANTE B	Me llamo Pedro.
ESTUDIANTE A	Mucho gusto.
ESTUDIANTE B	Igualmente.

1. José	5. Juan	9. Pedro
2. Susan	6. Ana	10. Tomás
3. Jack	7. Lola	
4. Paco	8. Miguel	

B. Work with a partner. Ask and answer: From where are you? I'm from . . . Follow the model.

(Pedro / México / mexicano)

ESTUDIANTE A	¿De dónde eres, Pedro?
ESTUDIANTE B	Soy de México. Soy mexicano.

1. José / Guatemala	4. Paco / Colombia	8. Miguel / Ecuador	12. Jorge / México
2. Susan / Chicago	5. Lola / Cuba	9. Pedro / Panamá	
3. Jack / Los Estados Unidos	6. Juan / Texas	10. Tomás / El Salvador	
	7. Ana / Costa Rica	11. María / Honduras	

C. Work with a partner. Ask and answer: From where is . . . ? He's from . . . Follow the model.

(Javier / Chile)

ESTUDIANTE A	¿De dónde es Javier?
ESTUDIANTE B	Javier es de Chile. Es chileno.

1. José / Guatemala	4. Paco / Colombia	8. Miguel / Ecuador	12. Jorge / México
2. Susan / Chicago	5. Lola / Cuba	9. Pedro / Panamá	
3. Jack / Los Estados Unidos	6. Juan / Texas	10. Tomás / El Salvador	
	7. Ana / Costa Rica	11. María / Honduras	

REVIEW

Read the dialogue aloud with a partner and then translate it to English.

Mark:	Hola. ¡Bienvenidos!
Pablo:	Gracias.
Mark:	¿Cómo te llamas?
Pablo:	Me llamo Pablo.
Mark:	¿De dónde eres?
Pablo:	Soy de Acapulco. Soy mexicano.
Mark:	Pablo, quiero presentarte a Gloria.
Pablo:	Mucho gusto.
Gloria:	Igualmente.
Pablo:	¿De dónde eres, Gloria?
Gloria:	Soy de Guatemala. Soy guatemalteca.
Mark:	¿Hablas inglés, Pablo?
Pablo:	No.
Mark:	Estudio español.
Pablo:	Ah . . . sí . . .
Gloria:	. . . Pablo . . . ¡Mucho gusto!
Pablo:	Gracias. Adiós.
Mark:	Hasta luego.
Gloria:	Hasta mañana.

Read the dialogue aloud with a partner and then translate it to Spanish.

Mark:	Hello. Welcome!
Pablo:	Thank you.
Mark:	What's your name?
Pablo:	My name is Pablo.
Mark:	Where are you from?
Pablo:	I'm from Acapulco. I'm Mexican.
Mark:	Pablo, I want to introduce you to Gloria.
Pablo:	Nice to meet you.
Gloria:	Same to you.
Pablo:	Where are you from, Gloria?
Gloria:	I'm from Guatemala. I'm Guatemalan.
Mark:	Do you speak English, Pablo?
Pablo:	No.
Mark:	I'm studying Spanish.
Pablo:	Ah . . . yes . . .
Gloria:	. . . Pablo . . . Nice to meet you!
Pablo:	Thank you. Goodbye.
Mark:	See you later.
Gloria:	See you tomorrow.

Translate the following to Spanish:

1. Hi! How's it going? _____

2. Good morning! _____

3. Welcome! _____

4. What's your name? _____

5. Do you speak English? _____

6. Do you understand English? _____

7. I'm studying Spanish. _____

8. I speak Spanish a little. _____

9. How are you? Fine, and you? _____

10. Where are you from? _____

11. I'm from Guatemala. _____

    I'm Guatemalan. _____

12. I'm Honduran. _____

13. Nice to meet you. _____

14. Same to you. _____

15. My name is Steve. _____

CULTURE: NATIONALITIES AND TERMS

What's the best word to use when discussing your Spanish speaking employees? Hispanic? Latino? Mexican? Spanish? The best term to use would be the nationality of the person. If he is from Guatemala, he is Guatemalan. If she is from Mexico, she is Mexican.

The term "Latino" or "Latinos" is appropriate to use if you are referring to a group of Spanish speaking people from many different Latin American countries. It is used amongst the people. They refer to themselves as Latinos from Latin America. There is a popular women's magazine entitled *Latina*.

The term "Hispanic" is an English word meaning "of or pertaining to ancient Spain." It is an umbrella term that the United States Government, Census Bureau, and Fortune 500 corporations use to refer to people from many different countries in Latin America and Europe. It has become popular to use but often it is not considered politically correct.

An appropriate term to use for a person from the United States is "Anglo." A Spanish word for a United States citizen is "estadounidense."

Americanos or Norteamericanos are terms that refer to and encompass people from all of North America including Canada, the United States, and Mexico.

TEAM BUILDING TIP

Latinos are very patriotic. Hang their country's flag next the U.S. flag. Be sure and hang it high or secure it tightly. They are so popular they often disappear. Post a colorful map of Mexico or the country of your employees. Show genuine interest in their town or village. Tack in a piece of string into their exact city and attach it to a photo of them with their name.

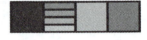

Training, Praise, and Question Words

PART I TRAINING PHRASES

Come with me.	**Ven conmigo.**
Watch me.	**Mírame.**
Do it like me.	**Hazlo como yo.**
Try it.	**Trátalo.**
Keep trying.	**Continua tratando.**
Help me.	**Ayúdame.**
It's necessary.	**Es necesario.**
It's important.	**Es importante.**
It's good.	**Está bien.**
It's bad.	**Está mal.**
It's so-so.	**Está así-así.**
It's correct.	**Está correcto.**
It's not correct.	**No está correcto.**
Everything else is perfect.	**Todo lo demás está perfecto.**
Good work!	**¡Buen trabajo!**
You're very strong!	**¡Eres muy fuerte!**
You're a hard worker!	**¡Eres muy trabajador!**

MATCHING EXERCISE

Write the letter of the Spanish word next to the English word it matches on the left.

1. _____ Watch me.
2. _____ Do it like me.
3. _____ Try it.
4. _____ Come with me.
5. _____ Help me.
6. _____ It's necessary.
7. _____ It's important.
8. _____ It's good.
9. _____ It's bad.
10. _____ It's correct.
11. _____ It's not correct.
12. _____ Everything else is perfect.
13. _____ Good work!
14. _____ You're a hard worker!
15. _____ You're very strong!

a. Ayúdame.
b. Está bien.
c. Está correcto.
d. ¡Eres muy trabajador!
e. Mírame.
f. Ven conmigo.
g. Está mal.
h. Hazlo como yo.
i. Es importante.
j. Trátalo.
k. ¡Eres muy fuerte!
l. ¡Buen trabajo!
m. No está correcto.
n. Es necesario.
o. Todo lo demás está perfecto.

CROSSWORD PUZZLES

Across

1. ¡Buen trabajo!
3. Házlo como yo.
7. ¡Eres muy fuerte!
8. Está mal.
11. Está correcto.

Down

2. Mírame.
4. Es necesario.
5. ¡Eres muy trabajador!
6. Es importante.
8. Está bien.
9. Trátalo.
10. No está correcto.

Across

1. ¡Buen trabajo!
3. Hazlo como yo.
7. ¡Eres muy fuerte!
8. Está mal.
10. Está bién.
11. ¡Eres muy trabajador!

Down

2. Mírame.
4. Es necesario.
5. Trátalo.
6. Es importante.
8. No está correcto.
9. Está correcto.

TRANSLATION EXERCISE

Translate the following to English:

1. Hazlo como yo. _____

2. Es necesario. _____

3. Trátalo. _____

4. Continua tratando. _____

5. Está correcto. _____

6. Ayúdame. _____

7. Ven conmigo. _____

8. Mírame. _____

9. Es importante. _____

10. ¡Eres muy trabajador! _____

11. Está bien. _____

12. Está así-así. _____

13. No está correcto. _____

14. Todo lo demás está perfecto. _____

_____

15. ¡Buen trabajo! _____

Translate the following to Spanish:

1. Try it. _____

2. Keep trying. _____

3. It's important. _____

4. You're a hard worker! _____

5. Help me. _____

6. It's good. _____

7. It's so-so. _____

8. Come with me. _____

9. Watch me. _____

10. It's necessary. _____

11. Do it like me. _____

12. It's not correct. _____

13. Everything else is perfect. _____

14. Good work! _____

15. You're very strong! _____

MULTIPLE CHOICE

Circle the letter of the correct answer.

1. **Come with me.**
   a. Está correcto.
   b. Ayúdame.
   c. Ven conmigo.
   d. Mírame.

2. **It's not correct.**
   a. Está correcto.
   b. Es importante.
   c. Está bien.
   d. No está correcto.

3. **Try it.**
   a. Hazlo como yo.
   b. Trátalo.
   c. Continua tratando.
   d. Ayúdame.

4. **Watch me.**
   a. Está correcto.
   b. Ayúdame.
   c. Ven conmigo.
   d. Mírame.

5. **Help me.**
   a. Está correcto.
   b. Ayúdame.
   c. Ven conmigo.
   d. Mírame.

6. **It's important.**
   a. Está correcto.
   b. Es importante.
   c. Está bien.
   d. No está correcto.

7. **You're a hard worker!**
   a. ¡Eres muy trabajador!
   b. No está correcto.
   c. Todo lo demás está perfecto.
   d. ¡Buen trabajo!

8. **Good work!**
   a. No está correcto.
   b. ¡Eres muy fuerte!
   c. ¡Buen trabajo!
   d. ¡Eres muy trabajador!

9. **Keep trying.**
   a. Hazlo como yo.
   b. Trátalo.
   c. Continua tratando.
   d. Ayúdame.

10. **Do it like me.**
    a. Hazlo como yo.
    b. Trátalo.
    c. Continua tratando.
    d. Ayúdame.

PART II   PRAISING BEHAVIOR

Perfect!	**¡Perfecto!**	Fabulous!	**¡Fabuloso!**
Incredible!	**¡Increíble!**	Fantastic!	**¡Fantástico!**
Excellent!	**¡Excelente!**	Magnificent!	**¡Magnífico!**
Exceptional!	**¡Excepcional!**	Marvelous!	**¡Maravilloso!**

MATCHING EXERCISE

Write the letter of the Spanish word next to the English word it matches on the left.

1. _____ Perfect!   a. ¡Excepcional!
2. _____ Incredible!   b. ¡Fabuloso!
3. _____ Excellent!   c. ¡Fantástico!
4. _____ Exceptional!   d. ¡Perfecto!
5. _____ Fabulous!   e. ¡Maravilloso!
6. _____ Fantastic!   f. ¡Excelente!
7. _____ Magnificent!   g. ¡Increíble!
8. _____ Marvelous!   h. ¡Magnífico!

CROSSWORD PUZZLES

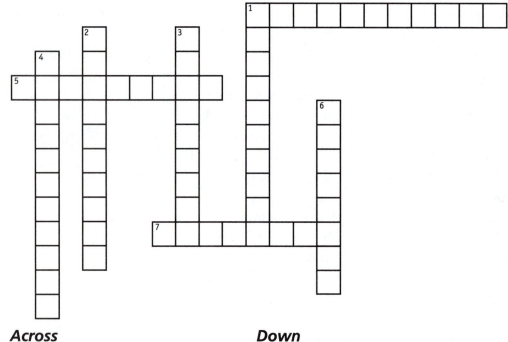

Across

1. Exceptional
5. Magnificent
7. Perfect

Down

1. Excellent
2. Fantastic
3. Incredible
4. Marvelous
6. Fabulous

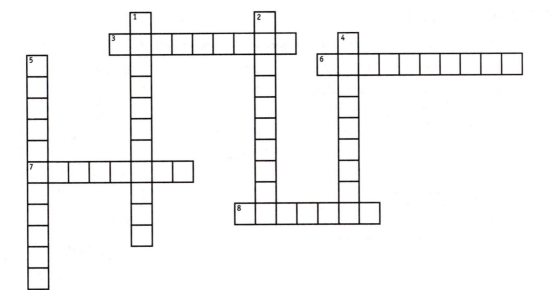

Across

3. Excelente
6. Maravilloso
7. Fabuloso
8. Perfecto

Down

1. Excepcional
2. Increíble
4. Fantástico
5. Magnífico

PART III   QUESTION WORDS

Where	**Dónde**
Where is	**Dónde está**
When	**Cuándo**
What	**Qué**
Who	**Quién**
With whom	**Con quién**
Why	**Por qué**
How	**Cómo**
How many	**Cuántos**

TEAM BUILDING TIP

Show your employees your appreciation of their hard work by awarding them with training certificates. Make sure the whole group receives one. They are group oriented and often do not like to be singled out. Shake hands with them, wish them congratulations, and snap a picture of them.

MATCHING EXERCISE

Write the letter of the word on the right next to the word it matches on the left.

1. _____ When   6. _____ Where   a. Cuántos   f. Cuándo
2. _____ What   7. _____ With whom   b. Quién   g. Por qué
3. _____ How many   8. _____ Why   c. Con quién   h. Dónde
4. _____ Where is   9. _____ How   d. Cómo   i. Dónde está
5. _____ Who   e. Qué

CROSSWORD PUZZLES

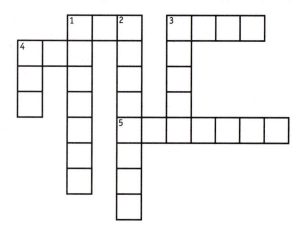

Across

1. Cómo
3. Cuándo
4. Quién
5. Dónde está

Down

1. Cuántos
2. Con quién
3. Dónde
4. Por qué

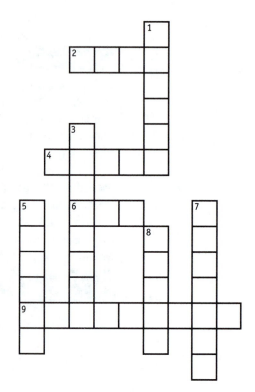

Across

2. How
4. Where
6. What
9. Where is

Down

1. Why
3. With whom
5. When
7. How many
8. Who

TRANSLATION EXERCISE

Translate the following to English:

1. Dónde _____

2. Cuándo _____

3. Quién _____

4. Dónde está _____

5. Con quién _____

6. Por qué _____

7. Cuántos _____

8. Qué _____

9. Cómo _____

Translate the following to Spanish:

1. Who _____

2. Where _____

3. How many _____

4. When _____

5. Where is _____

6. With whom _____

7. Why _____

8. How _____

9. What _____

MULTIPLE CHOICE

Circle the letter of the correct answer.

1. **When**
   a. Dónde
   b. Quién
   c. Qué
   d. Cuándo

2. **Where is**
   a. Con quién
   b. Por qué
   c. Dónde está
   d. Cómo

3. **Who**
   a. Cuántos
   b. Quién
   c. Qué
   d. Cuándo

4. **With whom**
   a. Con quién
   b. Por qué
   c. Dónde está
   d. Cómo

5. **What**
   a. Dónde
   b. Quién
   c. Qué
   d. Cuándo

6. **How**
   a. Con quién
   b. Por qué
   c. Dónde está
   d. Cómo

7. **Where**
   a. Dónde
   b. Quién
   c. Qué
   d. Cuándo

8. **How many**
   a. Quién
   b. Cuántos
   c. Qué
   d. Cuándo

9. **Why**
   a. Con quién
   b. Por qué
   c. Dónde está
   d. Cómo

REVIEW

Read the dialogue aloud with a partner and then translate it to English.

Jacky:	¡Hola Pablo!
Pablo:	Buenos días.
Jacky:	¿Cómo estás?
Pablo:	Bien, gracias.
Jacky:	Por favor . . . Ven conmigo.
Pablo:	Okay.
Jacky:	Es importante . . . Mírame.
Pablo:	(mira a Jacky)
Jacky:	Trátalo.
Pablo:	(lo trata . . . pero no tiene mucha confianza)
Jacky:	Hazlo como yo.
Pablo:	No está correcto . . .
Jacky:	Continua tratando.
Pablo:	(trata otra vez)
Jacky:	¡Excelente!
Pablo:	¿Está bien?
Jacky:	Sí. Todo lo demás está perfecto.
Pablo:	(tiene mucho orgullo)
Jacky:	Gracias. ¡Eres muy trabajador!

Read the dialogue aloud with a partner and then translate it to Spanish.

Jacky:	Hello Pablo!
Pablo:	Good morning.
Jacky:	How are you?
Pablo:	Fine, thank you.
Jacky:	Please . . . Come with me.
Pablo:	Okay.
Jacky:	It's important . . . Watch me.
Pablo:	(watches Jacky)
Jacky:	Try it.
Pablo:	(tries it . . . but is not very confident)
Jacky:	Do it like me.
Pablo:	It's not correct . . .
Jacky:	Continue trying.
Pablo:	(tries it again)
Jacky:	Excellent!
Pablo:	It's good?
Jacky:	Yes. Everything else is perfect.
Pablo:	(he is very proud)
Jacky:	Thank you. You're a hard worker!

Translate the following to Spanish:

1. It's important. _____

2. It's necessary. _____

3. Come with me. _____

4. Do it like me. _____

5. Perfect! _____

6. Fantastic! _____

7. Try it. _____

8. You're very strong! _____

9. It's good. It's bad. _____

10. It's correct. It's not correct. _____

11. Everything else is perfect. _____

12. You're a hard worker! _____

13. Marvelous! _____

14. Help me. _____

15. Where is _____

16. Who _____

17. With whom _____

18. How many _____

19. Where _____

20. When _____

21. Please _____

22. Thank you _____

23. Welcome _____

24. How's it going? _____

25. What's your name? _____

26. My name is Rich. _____

27. Do you speak English? _____

28. I'm studying Spanish. _____

29. Where are you from? _____

30. I'm from Bolivia. I'm Bolivian. _____

31. Nice to meet you. _____

32. Where is Jesús from? _____

33. Jesús is from Guadalajara. _____

34. I'd like to introduce you to _____

35. See you later. _____

CULTURE: CULTURAL SENSITIVITIES

United States males have been conditioned since they were children to hide emotions because it was regarded as a sign of weakness. They bring this attitude into the business world as adults as they keep a "stiff upper lip." Toughness and a hard-nosed attitude are qualities which are respected and admired. It is generally understood that emotions and business do not mix; this enables United States managers to accept criticism of their work and to learn from their mistakes, without taking it personally. In the United States it is important to remember that in business your work may be criticized but not you personally.

United States workers suppress any sensitivity they may have. Examples of this thick-skinned attitude are evident in every working day. A superior may reprimand a subordinate quite sternly for an error he or she had committed, but a few minutes later the two may be found laughing together over a cup of coffee. All is forgotten and their personal relations are as amicable as ever. In short, emotions are considered to be personal, with no place in the tough world of business.

Latinos are highly sensitive to criticism because of a deep emotional response to everything which affects them personally. This includes criticism of their work. They are proud of their work and it shows. When their work is criticized, it is taken personally. When they are criticized, they are offended and will often shut the person out. They often will stop speaking to him or give him the cold shoulder/silent treatment. Because of this sensitivity, people often consider Latinos to be "thin-skinned."

3

The Calendar, Numbers, and Time

PART I   NUMBERS

Cardinals

0	cero	13	trece	25	veinte y cinco	80	ochenta
1	uno	14	catorce	26	veinte y seis	90	noventa
2	dos	15	quince	27	veinte y siete	100	cien
3	tres	16	diez y seis	28	veinte y ocho	200	doscientos
4	cuatro	17	diez y siete	29	veinte y nueve	300	trescientos
5	cinco	18	diez y ocho	30	treinta	400	cuatrocientos
6	seis	19	diez y nueve	31	treinta y uno	500	quinientos
7	siete	20	veinte	32	treinta y dos	600	seiscientos
8	ocho	21	veinte y uno	40	cuarenta	700	setecientos
9	nueve	22	veinte y dos	50	cincuenta	800	ochocientos
10	diez	23	veinte y tres	60	sesenta	900	novecientos
11	once	24	veinte y cuatro	70	setenta	1000	mil
12	doce						

Ordinals

first	primero
second	segundo
third	tercero

MATCHING EXERCISE

Write the letter of the Spanish word next to the number it matches on the left.

1. _____ 6	10. _____ 3	a. trece	j. diez y ocho
2. _____ 14	11. _____ 12	b. cero	k. uno
3. _____ 8	12. _____ 11	c. diez	l. quince
4. _____ 10	13. _____ 1	d. nueve	m. doce
5. _____ 15	14. _____ 16	e. diez y siete	n. catorce
6. _____ 0	15. _____ 9	f. seis	o. ocho
7. _____ 7	16. _____ 17	g. cuatro	p. dos
8. _____ 18	17. _____ 13	h. diez y seis	q. once
9. _____ 2	18. _____ 4	i. tres	r. siete

MATCHING EXERCISE

Write the letter of the Spanish word next to the number it matches on the left.

1. _____ 20	6. _____ 40	a. treinta	f. diez
2. _____ 70	7. _____ 90	b. noventa	g. veinte
3. _____ 10	8. _____ 30	c. sesenta	h. cien
4. _____ 80	9. _____ 60	d. setenta	i. cincuenta
5. _____ 100	10. _____ 50	e. ochenta	j. cuarenta

MULTIPLE CHOICE

Circle the letter of the correct answer.

1. 80
   a. ochocientos
   b. ochenta
   c. ocho
   d. diez y ocho

2. 9
   a. nueve
   b. novecientos
   c. noventa
   d. diez y nueve

3. 100
   a. diez
   b. uno
   c. cien
   d. once

4. 2
   a. dos
   b. doce
   c. cien
   d. once

5. 300
   a. treinta
   b. tres
   c. trece
   d. trescientos

6. 50
   a. catorce
   b. cincuenta
   c. cinco
   d. quinientos

7. 3
   a. tres
   b. treinta
   c. trece
   d. trescientos

8. 18
   a. ocho
   b. diez y ocho
   c. ochenta
   d. ochocientos

9. 20
   a. veinte y dos
   b. nueve
   c. veinte
   d. treinta

10. 14
   a. cuatro
   b. catorce
   c. cuarenta
   d. cuatrocientos

ROLE PLAY

A. **El teléfono.** Your teacher will read off several of your telephone numbers. Raise your hand and answer "Hello" when you hear yours called!

B. **¡Muchos números!** Your organization got a new phone system. Take turns with a partner stating: Mi número de teléfono / fax / celular es el . . .

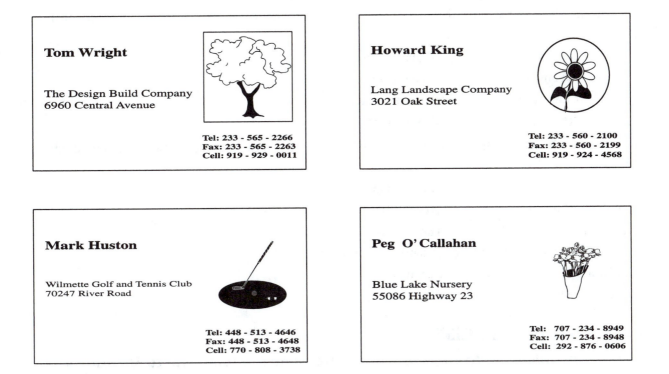

Tom Wright

The Design Build Company
6960 Central Avenue

Tel: 233 - 565 - 2266
Fax: 233 - 565 - 2263
Cell: 919 - 929 - 0011

Howard King

Lang Landscape Company
3021 Oak Street

Tel: 233 - 560 - 2100
Fax: 233 - 560 - 2199
Cell: 919 - 924 - 4568

Mark Huston

Wilmette Golf and Tennis Club
70247 River Road

Tel: 448 - 513 - 4646
Fax: 448 - 513 - 4648
Cell: 770 - 808 - 3738

Peg O' Callahan

Blue Lake Nursery
55086 Highway 23

Tel: 707 - 234 - 8949
Fax: 707 - 234 - 8948
Cell: 292 - 876 - 0606

C. **Mi número es . . .** Each student should ask the next student what his or her phone number is. One person should write the numbers on the chalkboard. If the recorder makes an error, the person whose number it is should correct it and then act as the recorder.

| ESTUDIANTE A | ¿Cuál es tu número de teléfono/fax/celular? |
| ESTUDIANTE B | Mi número es _____ . |

D. **Las direcciones.** Pretend your partner is your employee. Using the business cards tell him to go to work at those street addresses. Use *Vete a . . . Go to . . .* Then try expressing first (*primero*) and second (*segundo*) with the business locations.

SEVERAL REASONS TO USE NUMBERS

time
time sheets
money, paychecks
schedules
street addresses
telephone, fax, cell numbers
amounts
yardage and other
   measurements
price tags
equipment
golf course hole number

GRAMMAR: THERE IS, ARE

Hay can mean either "there is" or "there are."

There is a party.   **Hay una fiesta.**   There are ten pizzas.   **Hay diez pizzas.**

In a question, Hay can mean "Is there . . . ?" or "Are there . . . ?"

Is there beer?   **¿Hay cerveza?**   Are there CDs?   **¿Hay CDs?**

No hay means "there isn't any" or "there aren't any." In a question it means "Isn't there any?" or "Aren't there any?"

There isn't any music.	**No hay música.**
There aren't any pizzas.	**No hay pizzas.**
Isn't there any music?	**¿No hay música?**
Aren't there any pizzas?	**¿No hay pizzas?**

We use ¿Cuántos? and ¿Cuántas? to ask how many items there are. Sometimes muchos and pocos are used in the answer.

How many tacos are there?	**¿Cuántos tacos hay?**
There are thirty.	**Hay treinta.**
There are a lot.	**Hay muchos.**
How many pizzas are there?	**¿Cuántas pizzas hay?**
There are three.	**Hay tres.**
There are a few.	**Hay pocas.**

TRANSLATION EXERCISE

Translate the following to English:

1. Hay una fiesta. _____

2. Hay pizza. _____

3. No hay cerveza. _____

4. No hay música. _____

5. ¿Cuántos tacos hay? _____

6. ¿Cuántos burritos hay? _____

7. ¿No hay pizza? _____

8. Hay seis. _____

9. Hay pocos. _____

10. Hay muchos. _____

Translate the following to Spanish:

1. There is a party. _____

2. There is beer. _____

3. There is no pizza. _____

4. There is no music. _____

5. How many tacos are there? _____

6. How many burritos are there? _____

7. There are eight. _____

8. There are a lot of parties. _____

9. There are few pizzas. _____

10. Is there a lot of beer? _____

ROLE PLAY

A. **¿Muchos o pocos?** Your organization has asked you and a co-worker to help set up for the welcome dinner they are having for its new employees. Tell your partner whether there are a lot or only a few of the items shown. (Consider anything under six as few.)

Hay muchos tacos.

tacos	hamburguesas
burritos	cervezas
pizzas	platos
ensaladas	sandwiches

B. **¿Cuántos hay?** Using the picture in practice A, take turns asking and answering how many items of each picture there are on the table.

ESTUDIANTE A: ¿Cuántos burritos hay?
ESTUDIANTE B: Hay ocho.

PART II THE CALENDAR

Seasons—Las Estaciones

spring **la primavera**	summer **el verano**	fall **el otoño**	winter **el invierno**

Months of the Year—Los Meses del Año

January	**enero**	July	**julio**
February	**febrero**	August	**agosto**
March	**marzo**	September	**septiembre**
April	**abril**	October	**octubre**
May	**mayo**	November	**noviembre**
June	**junio**	December	**diciembre**

Days of the Week—Los Días de la Semana

Sunday	**domingo**	Thursday	**jueves**
Monday	**lunes**	Friday	**viernes**
Tuesday	**martes**	Saturday	**sábado**
Wednesday	**miércoles**		

Other Words—Otros Palabras

day	**el día**	night	**noche**
week	**la semana**	tomorrow morning	**mañana por la mañana**
month	**el mes**	tomorrow afternoon	**mañana por la tarde**
year	**el año**	tomorrow night	**mañana por la noche**
weekend	**el fin de semana**	every morning	**cada mañana**
today	**hoy**	every day	**cada día**
tomorrow	**mañana**	every afternoon	**cada tarde**
yesterday	**ayer**	every night	**cada noche**
morning	**mañana**	all the time	**todo el tiempo**
afternoon	**tarde**	only	**solamente**

MATCHING EXERCISE

Write the letter of the Spanish word next to the English word it matches on the left.

1. _____ November
2. _____ July
3. _____ January
4. _____ August
5. _____ fall
6. _____ September
7. _____ June
8. _____ winter

9. _____ February
10. _____ October
11. _____ summer
12. _____ spring
13. _____ April
14. _____ May
15. _____ March
16. _____ December

a. mayo
b. febrero
c. invierno
d. junio
e. abril
f. octubre
g. noviembre
h. diciembre

i. agosto
j. julio
k. primavera
l. marzo
m. verano
n. otoño
o. enero
p. septiembre

CROSSWORD PUZZLES

Across

6. September
7. April
8. March
9. October
11. January
12. July

Down

1. November
2. August
3. December
4. February
5. May
10. June

Across

2. junio
3. marzo
5. abril
7. enero
9. septiembre
10. noviembre
11. octubre

Down

1. febrero
3. mayo
4. julio
6. agosto
8. diciembre

TRANSLATION EXERCISE

Translate the following to Spanish:

1. February _____
2. April _____
3. May _____
4. June _____
5. August _____
6. October _____
7. November _____
8. January _____
9. March _____
10. July_____
11. September _____
12. December _____

Translate the following to Spanish:

1. spring_____
2. summer _____

3. fall _____
4. winter _____

ROLE PLAY

A. **Payday!** For financial planning purposes your organization has given out a calendar of paydays. Working with a partner give the dates. Follow the model.

(May 5, May 15)

ESTUDIANTE A: el cinco de mayo
ESTUDIANTE B: el quince de mayo

1. January 10, 24
2. February 8, 22
3. March 2, 13
4. April 6, 19
5. May 10, 24
6. June 16, 30

7. July 12, 28
8. August 8, 31
9. September 17, 29
10. October 9, 19
11. November 4, 14
12. December 3, 13

B. **When's your birthday?** Working in groups of four or five, ask and answer when each other's birthdays are. Follow the model.

ESTUDIANTE A: ¿Cuándo es tu cumpleaños?
ESTUDIANTE B: Mi cumpleaños es el 3 de mayo.

C. **Line up.** Work with the entire class. Stand up and ask one another: "¿Cuándo es tu cumpleaños?" and then form a line according to the order of your birthdays starting with January 1 and ending with December 31. See if you did it correctly by having the first January birthday call off his/her date in Spanish until the line ends!

MATCHING EXERCISE

Write the letter of the Spanish word next to the English word it matches on the left.

1. _____ Friday
2. _____ Tuesday
3. _____ Saturday
4. _____ Thursday
5. _____ Sunday
6. _____ Wednesday
7. _____ Monday
8. _____ day

9. _____ month
10. _____ week
11. _____ year
12. _____ today
13. _____ tomorrow
14. _____ weekend
15. _____ yesterday

a. hoy
b. lunes
c. sábado
d. miércoles
e. año
f. martes
g. viernes
h. ayer

i. fin de semana
j. jueves
k. domingo
l. semana
m. mañana
n. día
o. mes

CROSSWORD PUZZLES

Across

3. Sunday
5. Friday
6. Saturday
7. Wednesday

Down

1. Monday
2. Thursday
4. Tuesday

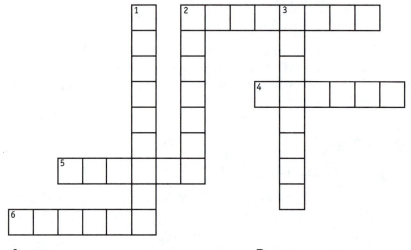

Across

2. jueves
4. domingo
5. lunes
6. viernes

Down

1. miércoles
2. martes
3. sábado

TRANSLATION EXERCISE

Translate the following to Spanish:

1. Sunday_____

2. Friday_____

3. Thursday_____

4. Monday _____

5. Saturday_____

6. Tuesday _____

7. Wednesday_____

Translate the following to Spanish:

1. today _____

2. tomorrow _____

3. morning_____

4. afternoon_____

5. day _____

6. weekend_____

7. everyday_____

8. every afternoon _____

9. every morning_____

10. only _____

MULTIPLE CHOICE

Circle the letter of the correct answer:

1. **Sunday**
   a. domingo
   b. sábado
   c. jueves
   d. viernes

2. **Friday**
   a. martes
   b. jueves
   c. viernes
   d. domingo

3. **Wednesday**
   a. sábado
   b. lunes
   c. jueves
   d. miércoles

4. **Tuesday**
   a. domingo
   b. jueves
   c. viernes
   d. martes

5. **Monday**
   a. sábado
   b. lunes
   c. jueves
   d. miércoles

6. **Thursday**
   a. domingo
   b. jueves
   c. viernes
   d. martes

7. **Saturday**
   a. sábado
   b. lunes
   c. domingo
   d. miércoles

ROLE PLAY

Go to . . . Pretend your partner is your co-worker. Using Vete (Go to) take turns telling each other where to go on the days indicated. To express "on," use "el." Follow the model.

1195 Asbury Street (Mon-Tues)
Vete a 1195 Asbury el lunes y martes.

1. 2303 Madison Street (Mon-Wed-Fri)

2. 369 Brown Avenue (Tues-Thurs)

3. 5500 Route 43 (Mon-Tues-Wed)

4. 450 Highway 83 (Thurs-Fri-Sat)

5. Number 16, 17, 18 (Mon-Wed-Fri)

6. 290 Sassafras Road (Mon-Thurs-Sat)

7. 700 Highway 55 (Fri-Sat)

8. 782 Hinman Street (Mon-Wed-Fri)

9. 9115 Hunter Boulevard (Tues-Thurs-Fri)

10. Number 7, 8, 9 (Tues-Sat)

PART III TELLING TIME

In expressing the time of day, "It is" is expressed by Es la una (It's one o'clock), and Son las dos, tres . . . for the plural hours (It's two o'clock, three o'clock, etc.).

It is one o'clock.	**Es la una.**
It is two (three, etc.) o'clock.	**Son las dos (tres, etc.).**

Time after the Hour is Expressed by the Hour + y, Followed by the Number of Minutes. Half Past is Expressed by y Media and a Quarter Past is Expressed by y Cuarto.

It's 1:10.	**Es la una y diez.**
It's 2:20.	**Son las dos y veinte.**
It's 3:15.	**Son las tres y cuarto. (or y quince.)**
It's 5:30.	**Son las cinco y media. (or y treinta.)**

At 8:00 . . . At 9:00, etc., would be a Las Ocho . . . A Las Nueve, etc.

At what time is . . .	**¿A qué hora es . . .?**
At what time is the party?	**¿A qué hora es la fiesta?**
The party is at 6:00.	**La fiesta es a las seis.**

Time Expressions

What time is it?	**¿Qué hora es?**	at night	**por la noche**
It's five o'clock.	**Son las cinco.**	on time	**a tiempo**
At what time is . . .	**¿A qué hora es . . . ?**	exactly, sharp	**en punto**
At 2:00, 3:00 . . .	**A las dos, tres . . .**	late	**tarde**
in the morning	**por la mañana**	early	**temprano**
in the afternoon	**por la tarde**	all the time	**todo el tiempo**

MATCHING EXERCISE

Write the letter of the Spanish phrase, on the right, next to the English phrase it matches on the left.

1. _____ It's 2:00.
2. _____ At 2:00
3. _____ It's 10:00.
4. _____ At 10:00
5. _____ What time is it?
6. _____ It's 6:30.
7. _____ At 6:30

8. _____ At what time is?
9. _____ in the morning
10. _____ in the afternoon
11. _____ early
12. _____ late
13. _____ on time
14. _____ exactly, sharp

a. temprano
b. A las dos
c. Son las diez.
d. A tiempo
e. ¿Qué hora es?
f. Son las dos.
g. tarde

h. en punto
i. Son las seis y media.
j. A las diez
k. de la tarde
l. ¿A qué hora es?
m. de la mañana
n. A las seis y media

CROSSWORD PUZZLE

Across

5. por la mañana
6. por la noche
8. temprano
9. tarde

Down

1. ¿Qué hora es?
2. por la tarde
3. a tiempo
4. en punto
7. todo el tiempo

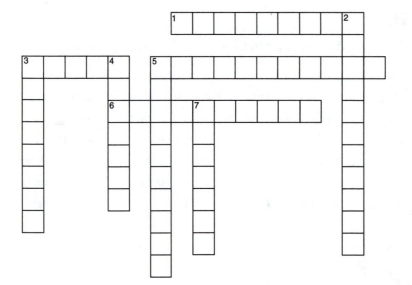

Across

1. What time is it?
3. late
5. in the morning
6. at night

Down

2. It's five o'clock.
3. early
4. exactly
5. in the afternoon
7. on time

MULTIPLE CHOICE

Circle the letter of the correct answer.

1. **all the time**
   a. todo el tiempo
   b. en punto
   c. tarde
   d. temprano

2. **It's 7:00.**
   a. A las seis.
   b. Son las seis.
   c. Son las siete.
   d. A las siete.

3. **It's 8:00.**
   a. Son las dos.
   b. Son las ocho.
   c. A las dos.
   d. A las ocho.

4. **at 9:00**
   a. son las nueve y diez.
   b. a las nueve y doce
   c. son las nueve y once.
   d. a las nueve

5. **at 6:30**
   a. son las siete y media.
   b. a las seis y media
   c. son las seis y media.
   d. a las siete y media

6. **What time is it?**
   a. ¿Qué hora es?
   b. ¿A qué hora?
   c. ¿Cómo estás?
   d. ¿Qué tal?

7. **It's 3:00.**
   a. Son las cinco.
   b. Son las tres.
   c. Son las tres y media.
   d. Son las dos.

8. **exactly, sharp**
   a. tarde
   b. de nada
   c. temprano
   d. en punto

9. **It's 1:00.**
   a. Es la una.
   b. Son las once.
   c. A las once.
   d. A la una.

10. **late**
    a. temprano
    b. tarde
    c. tiempo
    d. ahora

ROLE PLAY

A. **¿Qué hora es?** Working with a partner, ask and answer what time it is. Follow the model.

ESTUDIANTE A: ¿Qué hora es?
ESTUDIANTE B: Son las tres y media.

1. 2:00
2. 5:00
3. 7:00
4. 11:00

5. 9:30
6. 8:30
7. 4:30
8. 11:30

9. 7:45
10. 5:45
11. 3:45
12. 6:45

B. **¿A qué hora?** Pretend it's the first day of classes and seminars. Take turns asking and answering at what time the courses take place. Follow the model.

ESTUDIANTE A: ¿A qué hora es la clase de arte?
ESTUDIANTE B: A las dos.

8:00	Historia	1:10	Arte
9:30	Español	2:55	Comunicación
11:15	Inglés	4:30	Matemáticas

REVIEW

Translate the following to Spanish:

1. There are seven days in a week. _____
2. There are four weeks in a month. _____
3. There are four seasons in a year. _____
4. When is your birthday? _____
5. My birthday is May 24. _____
6. Go to Woodland Place on Monday, Tuesday, and Wednesday. _____
7. Go to Maple Apartments on Tuesday and Thursday. _____
8. Go to Oakdale on Monday, Wednesday, and Friday. _____
9. First, go to Old Orchard. _____
10. Second, go to Hoffman Estates. _____
11. What time is it? _____
12. It's 2:00. It's 5:30. _____
13. At what time is the party (la fiesta)? _____
14. The party is at 7:30. _____
15. The party is on Saturday! _____

Translate the following to Spanish:

1. How's it going? _____
2. How are you? _____
3. Welcome. _____
4. How's your family? _____
5. What's your name? _____
6. See you later. _____
7. I'd like to introduce you to _____
8. Where are you from? _____
9. Do you speak English? _____
10. Come with me. _____
11. Watch me. _____
12. Do it like me. _____
13. Help me. _____
14. It's important. _____
15. You're a hard worker! _____

Read the dialogue aloud with a partner and then translate it to English.

¡Bienvenidos!	¡Fiesta!
Qué:	¡Una Celebración!
Cuándo:	sábado, 3 de marzo
	A las 6:00
Dónde:	1620 Highland
Quién:	Mark
Oficina:	770-845-6293
Cell:	770-292-5856

Gloria:	¡Hay una fiesta!
Pablo:	¡Fantástico! ¿Cuándo es?
Gloria:	El sábado . . . el 3 de marzo.
Pablo:	¿Dónde está la fiesta?
Gloria:	5600 Sherman Avenue.
Pablo:	¿A qué hora?
Gloria:	A las seis.

El sábado a la fiesta . . . hay mucha música . . .

Mark:	Hola. ¡Bienvenidos!
Gloria:	Gracias.
Pablo:	¿Qué tal?
Mark:	¡Magnífico!
Mark:	Quiero presentarte a Octavio.
Gloria:	Mucho gusto.
Octavio:	Igualmente.
Gloria:	¿De dónde eres, Octavio?
Octavio:	Soy de Oaxaca. Soy mexicano.
Gloria:	¿Hablas inglés?
Octavio:	Sí. ¿Hablas inglés, Gloria?
Gloria:	Estudio inglés.
Mark:	Estudio español.
Octavio:	¡Perfecto! ¿Dónde está la cerveza?

(los dirige a la cocina)

Gloria:	¡Increíble!
Pablo:	Hay pizza y ensalada.
Gloria:	Sí . . . ¡Y hay muchos tacos y burritos!
Octavio:	Primero . . . ¡Una cerveza!

Read the dialogue aloud with a partner and then translate it to English.

Welcome!	Party!
What:	A Celebration!
When:	Saturday, March 3
	At 6:00
Where:	1620 Highland
Who:	Mark
Office:	770-845-6293
Cell:	770-292-5856

Gloria:	There is a party!
Pablo:	Fantastic! When is it?
Gloria:	On Saturday . . . March 3.
Pablo:	Where is the party?
Gloria:	5600 Sherman Avenue.
Pablo:	At what time?
Gloria:	At 6:00.

On Saturday at the party . . . there is a lot of music . . .

Mark:	Hello. Welcome!
Gloria:	Thank you.
Pablo:	How's it going?
Mark:	Magnificent!
Mark:	I want to introduce you to Octavio.
Gloria:	Nice to meet you.
Octavio:	Same to you.
Gloria:	Where are you from, Octavio?
Octavio:	I'm from Oaxaca. I'm Mexican.
Gloria:	Do you speak English?
Octavio:	Yes. Do you speak English, Gloria?
Gloria:	I'm studying English.
Mark:	I'm studying Spanish.
Octavio:	Perfect! Where is the beer?

(directs them to the kitchen)

Gloria:	Incredible!
Pablo:	There is pizza and salad.
Gloria:	Yes . . . And there are many tacos and burritos!
Octavio:	First . . . A beer!

CULTURE: TIME MANAGEMENT

When people from the United States and Latin American countries work together, one of the greatest difficulties, in addition to communication, is their pace of life. Cultures treat time very differently. One must realize that for employees coming from another country where time is looked upon differently, that they may find this pace to be one of their most difficult things to adapt to in the United States.

Since "time is money" in the United States and since money is what business is concerned with—all decisions, all activities, all commitments—be it at home or at work—are controlled by the clock. The employee is always under pressure to meet time commitments. Lack of punctuality is thought to be almost a disgrace. Business and pleasure progress by the clock. United States citizens are often said to be "slaves to nothing but the clock."

People in the United States place a high value on arriving at each meeting at exactly the designated hour. Punctuality is equated with reliability and efficiency, both meaningful values in U.S. culture, whereas late arrival and tardiness, suggest the opposite.

Many Latinos go about their lives without a daily and hourly calendar. The United States idea of using an appointment book to plan each day's activities into exact hourly blocks of time, is still unfamiliar to many Latinos. In their eyes, this would probably not allow for a natural flow of events.

While a United States citizen standing in line at the supermarket might be extremely aware of having to wait four or five minutes, a Latino would most likely be talking with a friend or just waiting patiently and politely. From the Latino perspective, impatient United States citizens may seem impolite, abrupt, or even obnoxious. In a Latino society, that values politeness over efficiency, open displays of impatience are usually always counterproductive.

The relaxed feeling toward time is starting to change among modern Latin professionals. As people's lives become more complex and pressures for improved productivity increase, people are starting to feel more concern for punctuality, and time appointments are more often met. But this is a gradual process, and the general feeling still is "what we don't get done today will keep until mañana." Such extreme awareness of the clock does not come naturally to most Latinos, who favor a more easygoing approach to life.

TEAM BUILDING TIP

Just as people in the United States would not like to work on holidays or on Super Bowl Sunday, for example, your Spanish-speaking employees don't want to work on their special holidays, either. Find out which ones they celebrate and don't forget to recognize them with a greeting card or a bouquet of flowers. Examples: La Virgen de Guadalupe, World Cup Soccer, Independence Days (see Chapter 12 for other important days). Mark your calendar and plan a celebration!

CHAPTER

4

Family and Work Personnel

PART I   FAMILY

family
la familia

grandparents
los abuelos

parents
los padres

mother
la madre

father
el padre

son
el hijo

daughter
la hija

children
los hijos

brother
el hermano

sister
la hermana

wife
la esposa

husband
el esposo

aunt
la tía

uncle
el tío

cousin
el (la) primo(a)

THE ARTICLE "THE"

In English, there is only one word for the word "the." In Spanish, there are four forms: la, las, el, los. They are the singular and plural, feminine and masculine forms. In English, we do not have the concept of feminine and masculine nouns; things are neuter.

	Singular	*Plural*
Feminine	la	las
Masculine	el	los

Write the correct form of the article "the." The ending of the following words should match with one of the four forms you choose: la, las, el or los.

1. _____ tacos
2. _____ salsa
3. _____ burritos
4. _____ cervezas

5. _____ amigos
6. _____ fiestas
7. _____ patio
8. _____ margarita

MATCHING EXERCISE

Write the letter of each picture next to the Spanish word it matches.

a.

b.

c.

d.

e.

f.

g.

h.

i.

j.

k.

l.

1. _____ la tía
2. _____ el primo
3. _____ la familia
4. _____ los hijos
5. _____ la hermana
6. _____ el tío

7. _____ el hijo
8. _____ los abuelos
9. _____ la madre
10. _____ la esposa
11. _____ el padre
12. _____ el hermano

VOCABULARY EXERCISE

Write the Spanish word for each picture in the space provided.

1. _____

2. _____

3. _____

4. _____

5. _____

6. _____

7. _____

8. _____

9. _____

MATCHING EXERCISE

Write the letter of the Spanish word next to the English word it matches on the left.

1. _____ family
2. _____ brother
3. _____ cousins
4. _____ wife
5. _____ aunt

6. _____ husband
7. _____ grandparents
8. _____ uncle
9. _____ mother
10. _____ father

a. familia
b. primos
c. hermano
d. tío
e. tía

f. abuelos
g. esposa
h. padre
i. madre
j. esposo

CROSSWORD PUZZLES

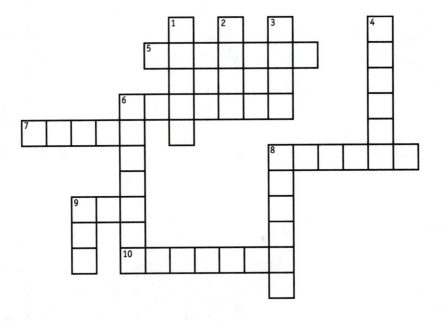

Across

5. family
6. brother
7. father
8. wife
9. aunt
10. grandparents

Down

1. mother
2. daughter
3. son
4. parents
6. sister
8. husband
9. uncle

Across

1. esposo
3. hija
5. hijo
6. tía
7. esposa
8. primo
10. madre

Down

2. hermano
4. abuelos
9. tío

TRANSLATION EXERCISE

Translate the following to English:

1. hermano _____
2. madre _____
3. primo_____
4. tío _____
5. familia _____
6. hermana _____
7. esposo _____
8. padre _____
9. hijo _____
10. abuelos _____

Translate the following to Spanish:

1. wife _____
2. sister _____
3. grandparents _____
4. family_____
5. brother_____
6. aunt _____
7. cousin _____
8. mother_____
9. father _____
10. daughter _____

MULTIPLE CHOICE

Circle the letter of the correct answer.

1. **father**
   a. el hermano
   b. el primo
   c. la madre
   d. el padre

2. **husband**
   a. el hermano
   b. el esposo
   c. el hijo
   d. el tío

3. **cousin**
   a. el hermano
   b. el primo
   c. la madre
   d. el padre

4. **mother**
   a. la madre
   b. la tía
   c. la hermana
   d. la hija

5. **grandparents**
   a. los hermanos
   b. los primos
   c. los abuelos
   d. los hijos

6. **aunt**
   a. la hija
   b. la madre
   c. la hermana
   d. la tía

7. **famliy**
   a. los abuelos
   b. los primos
   c. la familia
   d. la madre

8. **brother**
   a. el hermano
   b. el primo
   c. la madre
   d. el padre

9. **son**
   a. la hija
   b. el hijo
   c. el hermano
   d. la hermana

10. **wife**
    a. la hija
    b. la tía
    c. la hermana
    d. la esposa

ROLE PLAY

A. **What's her name?** In Chapter 1 you learned how to ask co-workers their names and state yours. Now, working with a partner, ask them the names of their family members in the photo. "Tu" means "your." "Mi" means "my." Follow the model.

(son / Raul)

ESTUDIANTE A: ¿Cómo se llama tu hijo?
ESTUDIANTE B: Mi hijo se llama Raúl.

1. mother / Margarita
2. brother / Guillermo
3. daughter / Raquel
4. sister / Cristina
5. son / Raúl
6. uncle / Samuel
7. father / Ignacio
8. grandfather / Ricardo

B. **How old is he?** Working with a partner, ask and answer how old the people are in the family photo. Follow the model.

(Raúl, 6)

ESTUDIANTE A:	¿Cuántos años tiene Raúl?
ESTUDIANTE B:	Raúl tiene seis años.

1. Margarita, 43   5. Raul, 6
2. Guillermo, 18   6. Samuel, 39
3. Raquel, 8   7. Ignacio, 55
4. Cristina, 22   8. Ricardo, 69

C. **How old are you?** Take turns asking and answering: How old are you? I am . . . Follow the model.

(Adam, 20)

ESTUDIANTE A:	¿Cuántos años tiene, Adam?
ESTUDIANTE B:	Tengo veinte años.

1. Marta, 18   5. Nancy, 50
2. Rodolfo, 72   6. Gustavo, 61
3. Bob, 34   7. Enrique, 83
4. Frank, 45   8. Sonia, 29

PART II   WORK PERSONNEL

boss
el jefe

secretary
la secretaria

foreman, crew leader
el mayordomo

crew
la cuadrilla

friends
los amigos

technician
el mecánico

manager
el (la) gerente

customer
el (la) cliente

woman
la mujer

man
el hombre

neighbor
el vecino

MATCHING EXERCISE

Write the letter of each picture next to the Spanish word it matches below.

a.

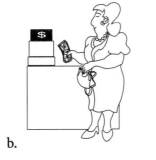

b.

c.

d.

e.

f.

g.

h.

i.

j.

1. _____ el jefe

2. _____ el (la) gerente

3. _____ el (la) cliente

4. _____ la mujer

5. _____ el mecánico

6. _____ la secretaria

7. _____ el mayordomo

8. _____ la cuadrilla

9. _____ los amigos

10. _____ el vecino

VOCABULARY EXERCISE

Write the Spanish word for each picture in the space provided.

1. _____

2. _____

3. _____

4. _____

5. _____

6. _____

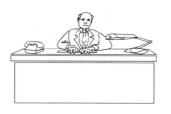

7. _____

8. _____

9. _____

10. _____

MATCHING EXERCISE

Write the letter of the Spanish word next to the English word it matches on the left.

1. _____ technician	a. mecánico
2. _____ secretary	b. mayordomo
3. _____ man	c. jefe
4. _____ boss	d. gerente
5. _____ neighbor	e. secretaria
6. _____ friend	f. amigo
7. _____ manager	g. cliente
8. _____ woman	h. mujer
9. _____ customer	i. hombre
10. _____ foreman	j. vecino
11. _____ crew	k. cuadrilla

CROSSWORD PUZZLES

Across

5. secretary
6. manager
7. neighbor
9. foreman, crew leader

Down

1. crew
2. friends
3. boss
4. woman
8. man

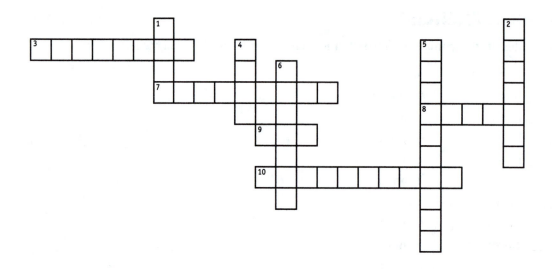

Across

3. vecino
7. secretaria
8. mujer
9. hombre
10. mecánico

Down

1. jefe
2. amigos
4. cuadrilla
5. mayordomo
6. gerente

TRANSLATION EXERCISE

Translate the following to English:

1. secretaria _____
2. mecánico _____
3. jefe _____
4. mayordomo _____
5. gerente _____
6. mujer _____
7. cuadrilla _____
8. hombre _____
9. amigo _____
10. cliente _____

Translate the following to Spanish:

1. crew _____
2. foreman _____
3. boss _____
4. friend _____
5. woman _____
6. customer _____
7. technician _____
8. secretary _____
9. manager _____
10. man _____

MULTIPLE CHOICE

Circle the letter of the correct answer.

1. woman
a. el jefe
b. el hombre
c. la mujer
d. la secretaria

2. crew leader
a. el mayordomo
b. el jefe
c. el vecino
d. el hombre

3. friends
a. la mujer
b. el hombre
c. la cuadrilla
d. los amigos

4. man
a. el jefe
b. el hombre
c. la mujer
d. el vecino

5. neighbor
a. el mayordomo
b. el jefe
c. el vecino
d. el hombre

6. boss
a. el mayordomo
b. el jefe
c. el vecino
d. el hombre

7. crew
a. la mujer
b. el hombre
c. la cuadrilla
d. los amigos

8. manager
a. el gerente
b. el jefe
c. el mayordomo
d. la mujer

9. technician
a. el mayordomo
b. la mujer
c. el hombre
d. el mecánico

10. secretary
a. el jefe
b. el hombre
c. la mujer
d. la secretaria

PART III   PERSONALITY TYPES AND EMOTIONS
GRAMMAR: COGNATES

Cognates are words that are the same or very similar in both English and Spanish. The following cognates describe people. (For men the words end in -o and for women they end in -a.)

aggressive	**agresivo, a**	intellectual	**intelectual**
ambitious	**ambicioso, a**	intelligent	**inteligente**
comical	**cómico, a**	introverted	**introvertido, a**
cooperative	**cooperativo, a**	materialistic	**materialista**
cruel	**cruel**	organized	**organizado, a**
extroverted	**extrovertido, a**	patient	**paciente**
generous	**generoso, a**	responsible	**responsable**
fair	**justo, a**	romantic	**romántico, a**
hardworking	**trabajador / trabajadora**	sensitive	**frágil**
honest	**honesto, a**	sincere	**sincero, a**
impatient	**impaciente**	sociable	**sociable**
impulsive	**impulsivo, a**	superstitious	**supersticioso, a**
independent	**independiente**	timid	**tímido, a**

VOCABULARY EXERCISE

A. Write your initials next to the characteristics that describe you.

agresivo, a _____	intelectual _____
ambicioso, a / _____	inteligente _____
cómico, a _____	introvertido, a _____
cooperativo, a _____	materialista _____
cruel_____	organizado, a _____
extrovertido, a _____	paciente _____
generoso, a_____	responsable _____
justo, a _____	romántico, a_____
trabajador _____	frágil _____
honesto,a _____	sincero, a _____
impaciente_____	sociable _____
impulsivo, a _____	supersticioso, a _____
independiente _____	tímido, a _____

B. Next, write the initials of one of your classmates or co-workers near the characteristics that describe him or her.

C. Now write the initials of your significant other near the characteristics that describe him or her.

GRAMMAR: I AM, YOU ARE, HE IS

to be	Ser
I am	Soy
You are	Eres
He, she is	Es

1. The verb *ser* means "to be." In Chapter 1 you learned three forms of *ser* to tell from where someone is.

I am from California.	**Soy de California.**
Where are you from?	**¿De dónde eres?**
Juan is from Honduras.	**Juan es de Honduras.**

2. We also use the verb *ser* to describe what someone is like.

I am comical.	**Soy cómica.**
You are ambitious.	**Eres ambicioso.**
María is intelligent.	**María es inteligente.**

How Much

very	**muy**
not very	**no muy**
a little	**un poco**
a very little	**un poquito***

*Poco and poquito are used for amounts. Pequeño, chico, and chiquito are used with sizes.

EXERCISES

A. Use these words and select ones from the cognate list to describe yourself.

Tell the following: 1) a characteristic you have a lot of, 2) one you have a little of, and 3) one you don't have.

1. Soy muy _____

2. Soy un poco _____

3. No soy muy _____

B. Next, describe one of your classmates or co-workers.

1. es muy _____

2. es un poco _____

3. no es muy _____

C. To say "You are" use the following pattern.

1. Eres muy _____

2. Eres un poco _____

3. No eres muy _____

D. Pretend this is a want ad. List the characteristics you need and want in an employee.

E. Fill in the blank with one of the cognates / characteristics.

1. Mi (My) mecánico es_____

2. Mi amigo es _____

3. Mi jefe es _____

4. El gerente es_____

5. La secretaria es_____

6. El mayordomo es_____

7. El hombre es _____

8. El cliente es _____

9. El vecino es _____

10. La mujer es _____

Emotions

How are you?	**¿Cómo estás?**	busy	**ocupado, a**
I am...	**Estoy...**	worried	**preocupado, a**
tired	**cansado, a**	sad	**triste**
confused	**confundido, a**	happy	**feliz**
content	**contento, a**	sick	**enfermo, a**
angry	**enojado, a**	good mood	**de buen humor**
furious	**furioso, a**	bad mood	**de mal humor**
nervous	**nervioso, a**		

MATCHING EXERCISE

Write the letter of the Spanish word next to the English word it matches on the left.

1. _____ good mood
2. _____ content
3. _____ happy
4. _____ sick
5. _____ tired
6. _____ sad
7. _____ angry
8. _____ busy

9. _____ worried
10. _____ bad mood
11. _____ furious
12. _____ nervous
13. _____ confused
14 _____ How are you?
15. _____ I am...

a. Estoy...
b. preocupado, a
c. triste
d. ¿Cómo estás?
e. feliz
f. de buen humor
g. de mal humor
h. confundido, a

i. contento, a
j. cansado, a
k. enojado, a
l. nervioso, a
m. furioso, a
n. enfermo, a
o. ocupado, a

CROSSWORD PUZZLES

Across

1. tired
6. angry
8. worried
9. sad
11. furious

Down

1. content
2. nervous
3. busy
4. good mood
5. bad mood
7. happy
10. sick

Across

2. nervioso
5. de mal humor
6. enfermo
8. enojado
11. cansado
12. ocupado

Down

1. de buen humor
3. feliz
4. preocupado
7. contento
9. furioso
10. triste

GRAMMAR: TO BE AND EMOTIONS

to be	**Estar**
I am	**Estoy**
You are	**Estás**
He, she is	**Está**

As you know when we want to ask how someone is feeling we ask *¿Cómo estás?* When we want to say how someone is feeling we also use the verb "Estar."

I am worried.	**Estoy preocupado.**
Are you nervous?	**¿Estás nervioso?**
The client is angry!	**¡La cliente está enojada!**

TRANSLATION EXERCISE

Translate the following to English:

1. Estoy enfermo._____

2. ¿Estás preocupado? _____

3. ¿Está enojado? _____

4. Estoy triste. _____

5. ¡Está furiosa! _____

6. Está ocupada._____

7. ¿Estás de mal humor? _____

8. Estoy confundido. _____

9. Estoy cansado. _____

10. ¿Está feliz? _____

11. ¡Estás de buen humor!_____

12. ¿Estás contenta? _____

Translate the following to Spanish:

1. Are you sick? _____

2. Is she angry? _____

3. I am worried._____

4. Are you confused? _____

5. You're in a good mood! _____

6. I am fine. _____

7. Are you busy? _____

8. He is happy._____

9. Are you tired? _____

10. He is in a bad mood. _____

11. She is furious! _____

12. I am nervous._____

MULTIPLE CHOICE

Circle the letter of the correct answer.

1. Are you sick?
   a. Está triste.
   b. ¿Estás enfermo?
   c. Está mal.
   d. Estás bien.

2. She is in a good mood.
   a. Está bien.
   b. Está de buen humor.
   c. Está contenta.
   d. Estoy contenta.

3. Is he angry?
   a. ¿Estás enojado?
   b. ¿Estás cansado?
   c. ¿Está enojado?
   d. ¿Estoy enojado?

4. Are you sad?
   a. ¿Estás triste?
   b. ¿Estás enojado?
   c. ¿Estás mal?
   d. ¿Estás enfermo?

5. I am worried.
   a. Estoy preocupado.
   b. Estoy ocupado.
   c. Estoy enojado.
   d. Estoy triste.

6. He is in a bad mood.
   a. Está enojado.
   b. Estoy mal.
   c. Estoy enojado.
   d. Está de mal humor.

7. Are you tired?
   a. ¿Estás contento?
   b. Estoy cansado.
   c. ¿Estás cansado?
   d. ¿Estás confundido?

8. Are you nervous?
   a. ¿Estás nervioso?
   b. Estoy nervioso.
   c. ¿Está nervioso?
   d. ¿Estás enojado?

9. She is furious!
   a. ¡Está furioso!
   b. ¡Está furiosa!
   c. ¡Estoy furiosa!
   d. ¡Estoy furioso!

10. Are you confused?
   a. Estoy cansada.
   b. Estoy confundida.
   c. ¿Estás confundida?
   d. ¿Estás contenta?

REVIEW

Translate the following to Spanish:

1. There are five children in my family. _____

2. There are four brothers. _____

3. What's your uncle's name? _____

4. What's your son's name? _____

5. How old is your daughter? _____

6. Christina is five years old. _____

7. My son is responsible and cooperative. _____

8. My manager is comical and organized. _____

9. The crew is hardworking. _____

10. The client is furious! _____

11. Are there problems? _____

12. I am nervous and worried. _____

13. My boss is angry! _____

14. The supervisor is in a good mood. _____

15. Are you sick? Sad? Confused? _____

Read the story aloud and then translate it to English.

Hola. Me llamo Octavio. Soy de Oaxaca, México. Soy mexicano. Tengo 22 años. Hay doce personas en mi familia. Tengo cuatro hermanos, dos hermanas, mis padres y cuatro abuelos. Estoy triste porque* mi familia está en México y estoy en Los Estados Unidos. Hablo español. . .no hablo inglés.
*porque – because

En Los Estados Unidos tengo muchos buenos amigos. Tengo muchas buenas amigas. ¡Gloria es la mujer que me interesa*!

Gloria trabaja** en White's Nursery. Gloria es generosa, sincera, cómica y muy romántica. Tiene 19 años. Es de Guanajato, México. Es inteligente. Gloria habla inglés un poco.

*Me interesa – interests me **trabaja – works

La familia de Gloria es grande. Gloria tiene tres hermanos en Los Estados Unidos. Su hermano es el mayordomo de mi cuadrilla. Se llama Manuel. Manuel tiene 25 años y es muy responsable, organizado y justo. Manuel habla inglés y español. Es bilingüe. Su hermano, Luis, tiene 23 años y es cooperativo, trabajador, y muy sencible. Luis está en mi cuadrilla. Su hermano, Raimundo, es el mecánico. Raimundo es cómico y siempre está de buen humor.

Read the story aloud and then translate it to Spanish.

Hello. My name is Octavio. I'm from Oaxaca, Mexico. I'm Mexican. I'm twenty-two years old. There are twelve people in my family. I have four brothers, two sisters, my parents and my four grandparents. I am sad because* my family is in Mexico and I am in the United States. I speak Spanish. . .I don't speak English.

*because – porque

In the United States I have many good friends. I have many good girlfriends. Gloria is the woman that interests* me!

Gloria works** at White's Nursery. Gloria is generous, sincere, comical, and very romantic. She is nineteen years old. She is from Guanajato, Mexico. She is intelligent. Gloria speaks English a little.

*interests me – Me interesa **works – trabaja

Gloria's family is large. Gloria has three brothers in the United States. Her brother is the foreman of my crew. His name is Manuel. Manuel is twenty-five years old and is very responsible, organized and fair. Manuel speaks English and Spanish. He is bilingual. Her brother, Luis, is twenty three years old and is cooperative, hard working, and very sensitive. Luis is on my crew. Her brother, Raimundo, is the mechanic. Raimundo is comical and always in a good mood.

Translate the following to Spanish:

1. Monday, Wednesday, Friday _____

2. Tuesday, Thursday, Saturday _____

3. March, June, August _____

4. January, December, September _____

5. There is salad, pizza, and beer. _____

6. Is there music? _____

7. What's your name? _____

8. My name is _____

9. I'd like to introduce you to _____

10. Where are you from? _____

11. Come with me. _____

12. Do it like me. _____

13. Try it. Keep trying. _____

14. You're a hard worker! _____

15. Good work! _____

16. It's important. It's necessary. _____

17. It's good. It's bad. It's so-so. _____

18. Everything else is perfect. _____

19. Where is the manager? _____

20. How many? _____

CULTURE: THE FAMILY

A common Spanish phrase "La familia sobre todo" addresses the importance given to the Latino family. It means "The family above all." Family takes priority over work and all other areas of life.

The strength of the Latino society continues to be the traditional family unit. It is often referred to as the "extended family" since it includes not only parents and children but aunts, uncles, cousins and grandparents as well.

Within the traditional family, the father is the undisputed authority figure as well as the disciplinarian. All important decisions are made by him. Traditionally, the mother is subordinate and seeks the advice and authority of him in all major concerns. She is presumed to be a devoted mother and dutiful wife and is highly valued as such. The parents are devoted to their children. Children are protected and cherished, and the typical weekend entertainment consists of the entire family, including grandparents, aunts, uncles, and cousins. Raised in these circumstances, children feel protected but are also very dependent on the help of their families.

When a child begins school, he/she normally goes along with the thinking of others, accepting the inflexibility of the school system. He/she now believes his teacher to be the undisputed authority and his inquisitive mind is suppressed. Because of this upbringing and education, when young employees arrive at the workplace, they seem submissive to their supervisor and accept instructions unquestioningly. Since they believe that their supervisor has complete authority, the subordinate's responsibility is restricted to completing the boss's job assignments.

The word "family" in the United States traditionally refers to simply parents and their children. In the typical United States family, the mother and father are considered co-authority figures.

In the United States, work often takes precedence over the family. The family is presumed to fit in around work schedules and activities. Employees are also counted upon to transfer their families if they get a job promotion. Families often relocate many times during their careers. Thus, family members are scattered and live in many different parts of the United States. Parents and siblings often only see one another a few times a year.

Divorce is commonplace. The present family condition and the loss of traditional family values (i.e. home-cooked family dinners every night) has caused much controversy over the years. The situation that has developed has placed extra burdens on the single parent who now has even less time available for the children because of the need to work full-time outside of the home.

A child brought up in this type of family, or where both parents work full time has had to do many tasks on his/her own. They have been responsible for many things at an early age. This type of person becomes self-sufficient, independent, and individualistic—characteristics that are considered positive in the United States. Because of this upbringing, young people arrive to a business organization full of self-confidence. They have many of the characteristics that are admired in an employee. They are independent thinkers, aggressive and competitive. They are comfortable sharing opinions with their supervisors as well as taking on positions of responsibility.

TEAM BUILDING TIP

Rent the movie, *La Familia*, from your local video store. It stars Jimmy Smits and it is a funny yet sad story about a Latino family. Enjoy a Mexican dinner while you watch it and don't forget a box of Kleenex. F.Y.I. There are only subtitles for the first five minutes!

CHAPTER

5

Rapport-Building Phrases

PART I   SPORTS

to play baseball
jugar al béisbol

to play basketball
jugar al básquetbol

to play football
jugar al fútbol americano

to play soccer
jugar al fútbol

to play tennis
jugar al tenis

to play golf
jugar al golf

to play volleyball
jugar al volibol

to play sports
jugar a los deportes

to play billiards
jugar al billar

to bowl
jugar al boliche

to fish
pescar

to swim
nadar

VOCABULARY EXERCISE

Write the Spanish word for each picture in the space provided.

1. _____

2. _____

3. _____

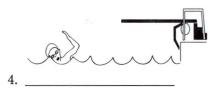

4. _____

5. _____

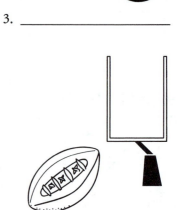

6. _____

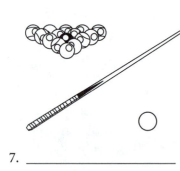

7. _____

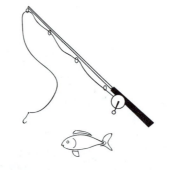

8. _____

9. _____

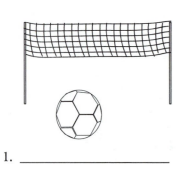

10. _____

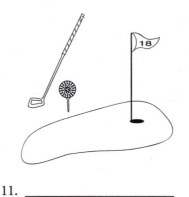

11. _____

12. _____

MATCHING EXERCISE

Write the letter of the Spanish phrase next to the English phrase it matches on the left.

1. _____ to play basketball
2. _____ to bowl
3. _____ to fish
4. _____ to play baseball
5. _____ to swim
6. _____ to play sports
7. _____ to play golf
8. _____ to play volleyball
9. _____ to play billiards
10. _____ to play soccer

a. jugar al volibol
b. jugar a los deportes
c. jugar al fútbol
d. pescar
e. jugar al boliche
f. jugar al basquetbol
g. jugar al béisbol
h. jugar al golf
i. nadar
j. jugar al billar

CROSSWORD PUZZLES

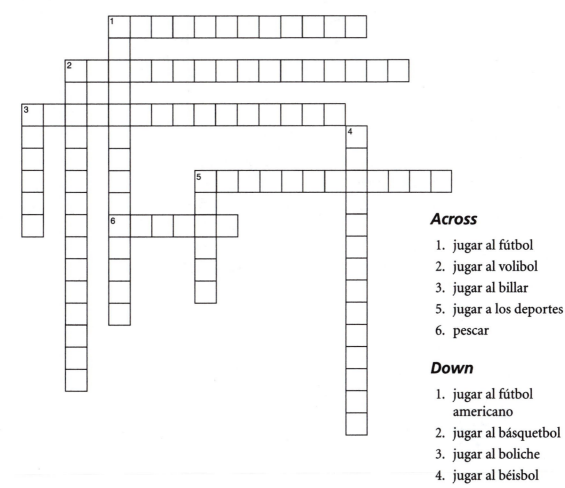

Across

1. jugar al fútbol
2. jugar al volibol
3. jugar al billar
5. jugar a los deportes
6. pescar

Down

1. jugar al fútbol americano
2. jugar al básquetbol
3. jugar al boliche
4. jugar al béisbol
5. nadar

Across

1. nadar
4. jugar al fútbol americano
6. jugar al tenis
8. jugar al boliche
9. jugar a los deportes

Down

1. jugar al básquetbol
2. pescar
3. jugar al fútbol
4. jugar al beísbol
5. jugar al billar
6. jugar al golf
7. jugar al volibol

TRANSLATION EXERCISE

Translate the following to English:

1. to play golf _____

2. to play sports _____

3. to play pool _____

4. to play soccer _____

5. to swim _____

6. to fish _____

7. to bowl _____

8. to play volleyball _____

9. to play basketball _____

10. to play tennis _____

GRAMMAR: Do you like to. . . ? / ¿Te gusta. . . ?

To ask someone's likes and dislikes, simply ask *¿Te gusta?* before the sports and activities you have learned.

Do you like to play soccer?	**¿Te gusta jugar al fútbol?**
Do you like to play baseball?	**¿Te gusta jugar al béisbol?**
Do you like to play golf?	**¿Te gusta jugar al golf?**
Yes, I like to go to parties.	**Sí, me gusta ir a fiestas.**
No, I do not like to go to parties.	**No, no me gusta ir a fiestas.**

One does not need to repeat the whole sentence. *Sí, me gusta* or *No, no me gusta* is also a correct way to respond in Spanish.

TRANSLATION EXERCISE

Translate the following to English:

1. ¿Te gusta jugar al volibol? _____

2. ¿Te gusta pescar? _____

3. ¿Te gusta nadar? _____

4. ¿Te gusta jugar a los deportes? _____

5. ¿Te gusta jugar al golf? _____

Translate the following to Spanish:

1. Do you like to play volleyball? _____

2. Do you like to swim? _____

3. Do you like to play tennis? _____

4. Do you like fish? _____

5. Do you like to play sports? _____

6. Do you like to play basketball? _____

7. Do you like to play baseball? _____

8. Do you like to play soccer? _____

9. Do you like to play billiards? _____

10. Do you like to bowl? _____

ROLE PLAY

A. **I like to or I love to. . .** Pretend you are working at a university campus with sports fields. Say whether you love (me encanta), like (me gusta), or don't like (no me gusta) to play the sport shown. Use one of the following phrases.

I love to play soccer.	**Me encanta jugar al fútbol.**
I like to play soccer.	**Me gusta jugar al fútbol.**
I do not like to play soccer.	**No me gusta jugar al fútbol.**

1.

2.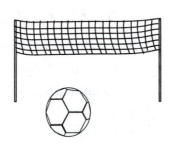

3.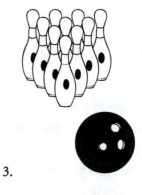

4.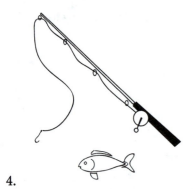

5.

6.

7.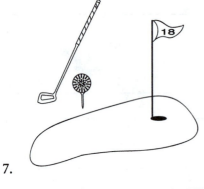

8.

9.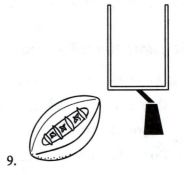

10.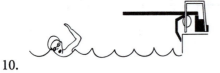

B. **What do you like to do?** Working with a partner, ask what activities he/she likes and does not like to do in each season. Follow the model.

ESTUDIANTE A: ¿Qúe te gusta hacer en la primavera?
ESTUDIANTE B: Me gusta jugar al béisbol pero no me gusta nadar.

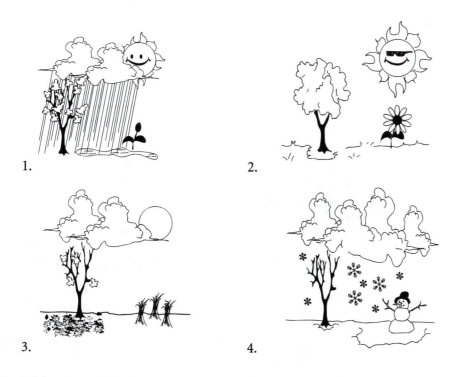

1.

2.

3.

4.

C. **With whom?** Working with a partner tell when and with whom you like play these sports. Follow the model.

summer/volleyball/friends   En el verano me gusta jugar al volibol con mis amigos.

1. baseball/brothers   2. football/supervisors   3. swim/children   4. basketball/uncle

5. soccer/technician   6. fish/boss   7. billiards/father   8. bowling/family

PART II   ACTIVITIES

to read
leer

to dance
bailar

to go to parties
ir a fiestas

to be with family
estar con familia

to play cards
jugar cartas

to drink
tomar, beber

to eat
comer

to listen to music
escuchar música

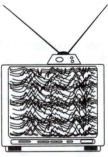

to watch television
mirar la televisión

MATCHING EXERCISE

Write the letter of each picture next to the Spanish word it matches below.

 a.

 b.

 c.

 d.

 e.

 f.

 g.

 h.

 i.

1. _____ bailar
2. _____ leer
3. _____ comer
4. _____ tomar, beber
5. _____ ir a fiestas

6. _____ mirar la televisión
7. _____ escuchar música
8. _____ jugar cartas
9. _____ estar con familia

VOCABULARY EXERCISE

Write the Spanish word for each picture in the space provided.

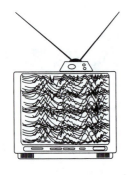

1. _____
2. _____
3. _____

4. _____
5. _____
6. _____

7. _____
8. _____
9. _____

MATCHING EXERCISE

Write the letter of the Spanish phrase next to the English phrase it matches on the left.

1. _____ to listen to music   a. tomar, beber
2. _____ to read   b. jugar cartas
3. _____ to dance   c. ir a fiestas
4. _____ to play cards   d. mirar la televisión
5. _____ to be with family   e. leer
6. _____ to watch television   f. estar con familia
7. _____ to eat   g. escuchar música
8. _____ to drink   h. comer
9. _____ to go to parties   i. bailar

CROSSWORD PUZZLES

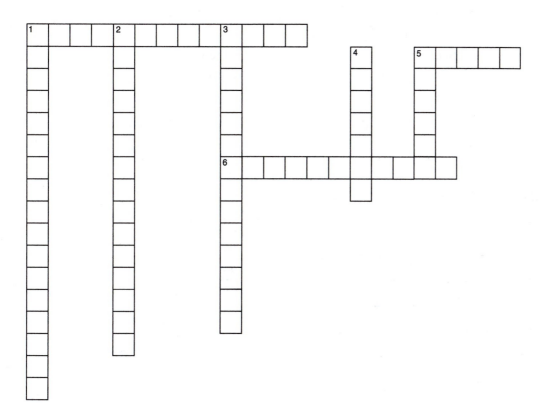

Across

1. ir a fiestas
5. comer
6. jugar cartas

Down

1. mirar la televisión
2. escuchar música
3. estar con familia
4. bailar
5. leer

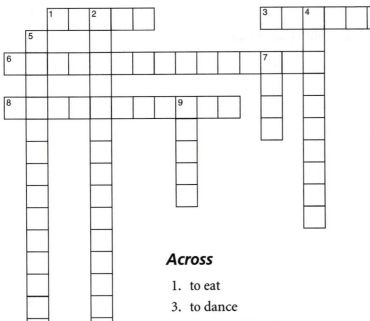

Across

1. to eat
3. to dance
6. to be with family
8. to play cards

Down

2. to watch television
4. to go to parties
5. to listen to music
7. to read
9. to drink

TRANSLATION EXERCISE

Translate the following to English:

1. ir a fiestas _____

2. mirar la televisión _____

3. bailar _____

4. estar con familia _____

5. tomar _____

6. comer _____

7. jugar cartas _____

8. escuchar música _____

9. leer _____

10. jugar al béisbol _____

Translate the following to Spanish:

1. to listen to music _____
2. to read _____
3. to dance _____
4. to drink _____
5. to eat _____
6. to go to parties _____
7. to watch T.V. _____
8. to be with family _____
9. to play cards _____
10. to play soccer _____

MATCHING EXERCISE

Circle the letter of the correct answer.

1. **to listen to music**
   a. mirar la televisión
   b. escuchar la radio
   c. escuchar música
   d. ir a fiestas

2. **to dance**
   a. nadar
   b. pescar
   c. jugar cartas
   d. bailar

3. **to play cards**
   a. jugar al billar
   b. jugar al volibol
   c. jugar al boliche
   d. jugar cartas

4. **to fish**
   a. pescar
   b. nadar
   c. tomar
   d. ir a fiestas

5. **to read**
   a. comer
   b. tomar
   c. bailar
   d. leer

6. **to bowl**
   a. nadar
   b. bailar
   c. jugar al boliche
   d. jugar al billar

7. **to play billiards**
   a. jugar al billar
   b. jugar al boliche
   c. comer
   d. bailar

8. **to swim**
   a. bailar
   b. comer
   c. nadar
   d. pescar

GRAMMAR: EXPRESSING I . . . AND DO YOU . . .?

You have learned to express your likes and dislikes using the verb *gustar*. To express that you actually take part in the activity, take off the –ar, -er, or –ir ending and add 'o' to the word. Study the model.

| I like to listen to music. | **Me gusta escuchar música.** |
| I listen to Jazz. | **Escucho Jazz.** |

To say that you do not take part in the activities, add "no" before the word.

| I dance. | **Bailo.** |
| I do not dance. | **No bailo.** |

To ask someone about what activities he/she participates in, take off the –ar, -er, or –ir ending and add "as" to the word.

Do you like to watch T.V.?	**¿Te gusta mirar la televisión?**
Do you watch *Friends?*	**¿Miras *Friends?***
Yes, I watch *Friends.*	**Sí, miro *Friends.***

Jugar "to play" is irregular.

| I play golf. | **Juego golf.** |
| Do you play volleyball? | **¿Juegas volibol?** |

TRANSLATION EXERCISE

Translate the following to Spanish:

1. I dance. _____

2. I swim. _____

3. I fish. _____

4. I drink. _____

5. I listen to music. _____

6. I play billiards. _____

7. I watch T.V. _____

8. I read. _____

9. I do not dance. _____

10. I do not swim. _____

11. I do not fish. _____

12. I do not drink. _____

13. I do not listen to music. _____

_____

14. I do not play billiards. _____

15. I do not watch T.V. _____

16. I do not read. _____

17. Do you dance? _____

18. Do you swim? _____

19. Do you fish? _____

20. Do you drink? _____

21. Do you listen to music? _____

_____

22. Do you play billiards? _____

23. Do you watch T.V.? _____

_____

24. Do you read? _____

25. Do you dance? _____

ROLE PLAY

A. **Always talking about work gets boring!** Find out more about your co-workers interests by asking if he/she participates in these activities. Follow the model.

ESTUDIANTE A:	¿Juegas tenis?
ESTUDIANTE B:	Sí, juego tenis. (No, no juego tenis.)

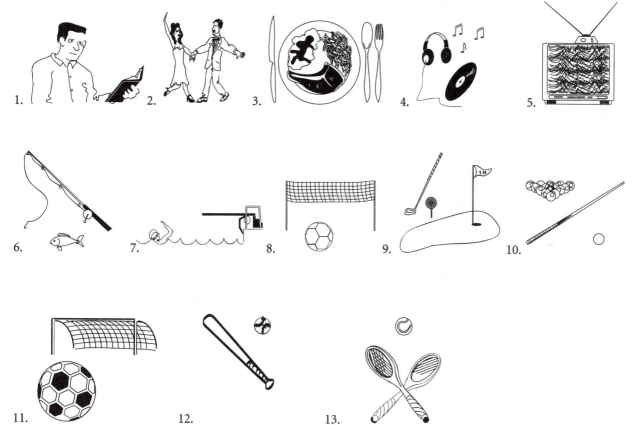

B. Now ask each other with whom (Con quién) they do the activities. Follow the model.

ESTUDIANTE A:	¿Con quién juegas tenis?
ESTUDIANTE B:	Juego tenis con mi amigo.

C. Working with a partner, ask and answer when (¿Cuándo) he/she does these activities. Follow the model.

ESTUDIANTE A:	¿Cuándo juegas tenis?
ESTUDIANTE B:	Juego tenis en el verano.

REVIEW

Translate the following to Spanish:

1. I like to read. _____

2. I like to be with my family. _____

3. I do not like to go to parties. _____

4. Do you like to play sports? _____

5. Do you like to watch television? _____

6. Do you like to play billiards? _____

7. I listen to music. Do you listen to music? _____

8. I do not watch television. _____

9. I watch golf with my father on Sundays. _____

10. I dance with my wife on Saturdays. _____

11. I play soccer with my supervisors in the fall. _____

12. I fish on the weekends with my friends. _____

13. I play golf in the summer with my boss. _____

14. When do you play volleyball? _____

15. When do you play baseball? _____

Read the dialogue aloud with a partner and then translate it to English.

(viernes, 22 de abril)

Gloria: ¡Hola, Octavio!

Octavio: Hola. ¿Qué tal?

Gloria: ¡Fantástico! ¡Es viernes!

Octavio: ¿Qué te gusta hacer los sábados?

Gloria: Me gusta estar con familia.

Octavio: Ah. . . ¿Te gusta jugar al fútbol?

Gloria: No. . . no me gusta.

Octavio: ¿Te gusta jugar al volibol?

Gloria: No. . . no me gusta jugar deportes.

Octavio: Ah. . . ¿Te gusta jugar al billar?

Gloria: Sí. . . un poco. ¿Hay música?

Read the dialogue aloud with a partner and then translate it to Spanish.

(Friday, April 22)

Gloria: Hello, Octavio!

Octavio: Hello. How's it going?

Gloria: Fantastic! It's Friday!

Octavio: What do you like to do on Saturdays?

Gloria: I like to be with the family.

Octavio: Ah. . . Do you like to play soccer?

Gloria: No. . . I don't like to.

Octavio: Do you like to play volleyball?

Gloria: No. . . I do not like to play sports.

Octavio: Ah. . . Do you like to play billiards?

Gloria: Yes. . . A little. Is there music?

(el sábado, 23 de abril en el bar) | (On Saturday, April 23 at the bar)

Octavio: Primero. . . ¿Tomas una Margarita?

Octavio: First. . . Do you want to drink a Margarita?

Gloria: No, gracias. No tomo.

Gloria: No, thank you. I do not drink.

Octavio: Me gusta tomar. Una Margarita, por favor. . .

Octavio: I like to drink. A Margarita, please. . .

Gloria: ¿Hay pizza? ¡ Me encanta comer!

Gloria: Is there pizza? I love to eat!

Sergio: ¡Hola! ¿Qué tal?

Sergio: Hello! How's it going?

Octavio: ¡Sergio! ¡Hola! ¿Como estás?

Octavio: Sergio! Hello! How are you?

Sergio: ¡Magnífico!

Sergio: Magnificent!

Octavio: ¿Cómo está la familia?

Octavio: How's the family?

Sergio: ¡Excelente! Gracias.

Sergio: Excellent! Thank you.

Octavio: ¿Y tus hermanos?

Octavio: And your brothers?

Sergio: Bien, gracias.

Sergio: Fine, thank you.

Octavio: Quiero presentarte a Gloria.

Octavio: I want to introduce you to Gloria.

Sergio: Mucho gusto.

Sergio: Nice to meet you.

Gloria: Igualmente.

Gloria: Same to you.

Octavio: ¡Hasta luego!

Octavio: See you later!

(Octavio y Gloria van a jugar al billar) | (Octavio y Gloria go to play billards)

Octavio: Ven conmigo, Gloria. . .

Octavio: Come with me, Gloria. . .

Gloria: Estoy nerviosa.

Gloria: I'm nervous.

Octavio: Mírame.

Octavio: Watch me.

Gloria: (le mira)

Gloria: (she watches him)

Octavio: Trátalo.

Octavio: Try it.

Gloria: (golpea mal la bola)

Gloria: (she hits the ball poorly)

Octavio: No está correcto. . . Hazlo como yo.

Octavio: It's not correct. . . Do it like me.

Gloria: Ayudame, Octavio.

Gloria: Help me, Octavio.

Octavio: Está así- así.

Octavio: It's so so.

Gloria: ¡No me gusta jugar al billar!

Gloria: I don't like to play billiards!

Octavio: Continua tratando. . . ¡Fabuloso!

Octavio: Keep trying. . . Fabulous!

Gloria: Eres paciente, Octavio.

Gloria: You are patient, Octavio.

Octavio: Todo lo demás está correcto.

Octavio: Everything else is correct.

Gloria: Muchas gracias. Octavio. . . ¿Te gusta bailar?

Gloria: Thank you very much. Octavio. . . Do you like to dance?

CULTURE: GROUP VERSUS INDIVIDUALISTIC CULTURES

In the United States people speak of "healthy competition." United States citizens have been competing since they were in elementary school in activities such as spelling bees and relay races. They went from those childhood games to competing for jobs. The United States thrives on the stimulus of competition. They enjoy a competitive environment and feel that it does, for the most part, make for high-quality performance, a healthy business, and a strong economy.

The phrases "play to win" and compete "head to head" and "one on one" are commonly heard. The United States is an individualist society. In the United States, rewards are for individual achievement. Common awards presented are "Employee of the Month," "Teacher of the Year" and "Most Valuable Player." Companies feel the need to hire in business consultants to facilitate "Team Building" seminars for their employees so that they learn to work together better as a group.

Working as a group comes naturally to many other cultures. In Latin America and much of the world, individual ties are very loose. People are born into collectives and groups that may be their extended family. The saying "It takes a village to raise a child" is now being realized as an important concept in the United States. People are very much involved in and gain their identity from the group. They feel that loyalty to the group should be highly rewarded. Most Latinos are very cooperative and work well with one another in the group. They are protective of the group as a whole and will often tell a supervisor they do not want a person in their group because he/she makes the group look bad.

The majority of Latino employees are not strongly competitive in the sense of wanting to surpass the performance of their co-workers. They find it unpleasant to step on their co-workers' toes to gain recognition for superior individual achievement. They would like to be in agreement with one another with no outright winners and losers. For example, in a soccer game, they are competitive, but at work they value a more friendly, relaxed atmosphere, free of conflict and confrontation. Latinos usually avoid competitions or volunteering for something which may show them in a negative light. They may fail at the task. In a close-knit and group-oriented Latino society, one's standing with friends and co-workers is very important.

TEAM BUILDING TIP

In Chapter 13 you will read about the H2B government immigrant labor program. One of the top five reasons H2B employees quit is the lack of evening entertainment. They are miles from their family and friends, and these activities would give them something to look forward to, rather than just working all the time.

Put up a basketball hoop and a volleyball net near your facility. Outline the boundaries with spray paint. You may not be able to communicate with your employees in Spanish well right now, but until you can communicate better with them in Spanish, at least you can play with them. Organize a soccer or a volleyball league with other organizations near you. Have them go out bowling or to a pool hall twice a month. Go to a baseball game together. Have you ever lived in a foreign country and felt the loneliness? Show your employees you care about them, and they will return year after year.

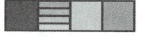

6

Health and Safety Phrases and Terms

PART I   HEALTH PHRASES AND TERMS

head
la cabeza

eye
el ojo

ear
el oído

neck
el cuello

shoulder
el hombro

chest
el pecho

stomach
el estómogo

leg
la pierna

knee
la rodilla

ankle
el tobillo

feet
los pies

back
la espalda

blood
la sangre

arm
el brazo

elbow
el codo

hand
la mano

fingers
los dedos

GRAMMAR

In Spanish we use the definite article "the" (el, la, los, las) when referring to parts of the body.

MATCHING EXERCISE

Write the letter of the picture next to the Spanish word it matches.

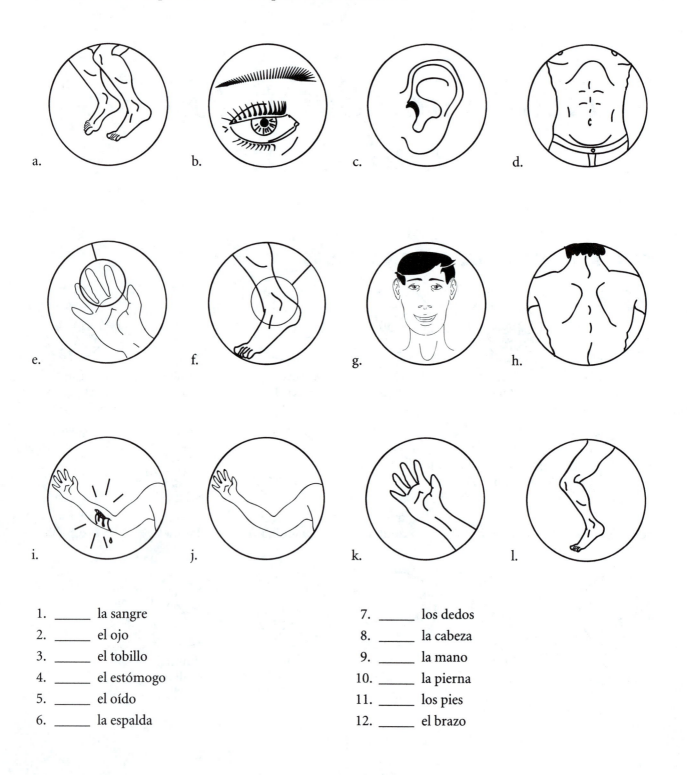

a.   b.   c.   d.

e.   f.   g.   h.

i.   j.   k.   l.

1. _____ la sangre
2. _____ el ojo
3. _____ el tobillo
4. _____ el estómogo
5. _____ el oído
6. _____ la espalda

7. _____ los dedos
8. _____ la cabeza
9. _____ la mano
10. _____ la pierna
11. _____ los pies
12. _____ el brazo

VOCABULARY EXERCISE

Write the Spanish word for each picture in the space provided.

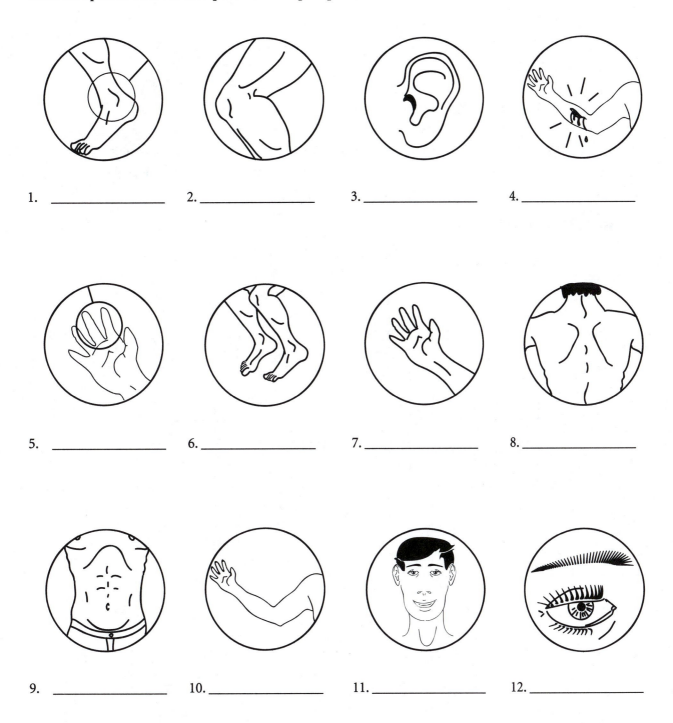

1. _____

2. _____

3. _____

4. _____

5. _____

6. _____

7. _____

8. _____

9. _____

10. _____

11. _____

12. _____

MATCHING EXERCISE

Write the letter of the Spanish word next to the English word it matches on the left.

1. _____ feet
2. _____ knee
3. _____ eye
4. _____ ear
5. _____ hand
6. _____ elbow
7. _____ ankle
8. _____ leg

9. _____ stomach
10. _____ arm
11. _____ head
12. _____ chest
13. _____ fingers
14. _____ back
15. _____ shoulder
16. _____ neck

a. la cabeza
b. el brazo
c. el estómogo
d. la pierna
e. el tobillo
f. los pies
g. la rodilla
h. la mano

i. el codo
j. el hombro
k. el cuello
l. el pecho
m. el oído
n. el ojo
o. los dedos
p. la espalda

CROSSWORD PUZZLES

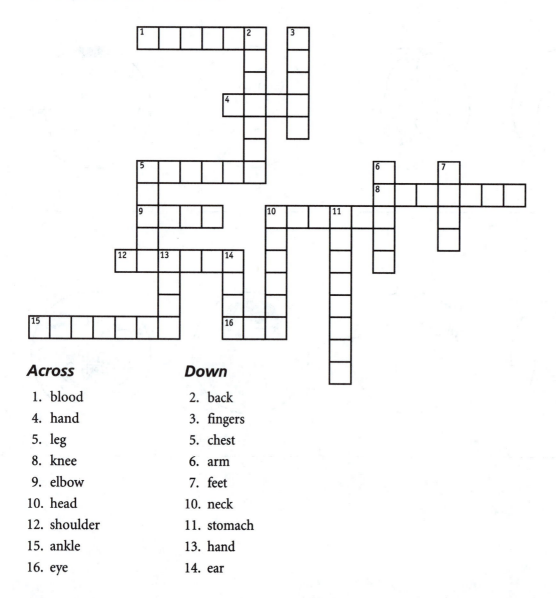

Across

1. blood
4. hand
5. leg
8. knee
9. elbow
10. head
12. shoulder
15. ankle
16. eye

Down

2. back
3. fingers
5. chest
6. arm
7. feet
10. neck
11. stomach
13. hand
14. ear

Across

1. cuello
3. espalda
5. hombro
7. rodilla
9. ojo
10. pies
11. brazo
12. pierna
13. sangre
15. mano
16. oído

Down

2. pecho
4. tobillo
5. estómogo
6. cabeza
8. codo
14. dedo

TRANSLATION EXERCISE

Translate the following to English:

1. los pies _____
2. la mano _____
3. la rodilla _____
4. los dedos _____
5. la cabeza _____
6. la sangre _____
7. el oído _____
8. el hombro _____
9. la espalda _____
10. el pecho _____
11. el brazo _____
12. el codo _____
13. la pierna _____
14. el tobillo _____
15. el ojo _____

Translate the following to Spanish:

1. feet _____
2. hand _____
3. fingers _____
4. blood _____
5. head _____
6. eye _____
7. arm _____
8. ear _____
9. shoulder _____
10. chest _____
11. back _____
12. ankle _____
13. knee _____
14. stomach _____
15. leg _____

MULTIPLE CHOICE

Circle the letter of the correct answer.

1. **fingers**
   a. los dedos
   b. los pies
   c. los brazos
   d. la pierna

2. **ankle**
   a. la rodilla
   b. la pierna
   c. el tobillo
   d. el brazo

3. **eye**
   a. la sangre
   b. la mano
   c. el oído
   d. el ojo

4. **head**
   a. la cabeza
   b. la espalda

   c. la pierna
   d. el hombro

5. **ear**
   a. el ojo
   b. el oído
   c. la rodilla
   d. el pecho

6. **back**
   a. la cabeza
   b. el pecho
   c. el estómogo
   d. la espalda

7. **blood**
   a. el pulgar
   b. el cuello
   c. el codo
   d. la sangre

8. **feet**
   a. los pies
   b. los dedos
   c. la cabeza
   d. la pierna

9. **hand**
   a. la mano
   b. el codo
   c. el pecho
   d. el tobillo

10. **knee**
    a. el brazo
    b. el tobillo
    c. la rodilla
    d. el cuello

GRAMMAR

In Spanish we use the definite article "the" (el, la, los, las) when referring to parts of the body. The verb *doler* means to hurt, to ache.

ROLE PLAY

Imagine that your co-worker has been hurt on the job. Ask what hurts the person. Follow the model.

ESTUDIANTE A: ¿Qué te duele?
ESTUDIANTE B: Me duele el tobillo.

1.  2. 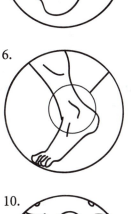 3. 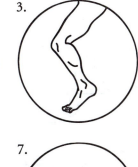 4.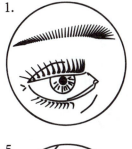

5.  6. 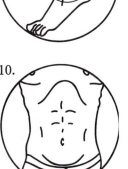 7. 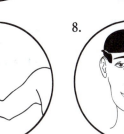 8.

9. 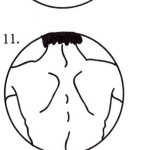 10. 11.

TRANSLATION EXERCISE

Translate the following to Spanish:

1. What hurts? _____

2. My head hurts. _____

3. My eye hurts. _____

4. What hurts? _____

5. My ankle hurts. _____

6. My knee hurts. _____

7. What hurts? _____

8. My stomach hurts. _____

9. My back hurts. _____

10. What hurts? _____

PART II SAFETY PHRASES AND TERMS

fire extinguisher
el extinguidor

first aid kit
el botíquín

earplugs
los tapones para los oídos

baseball cap
la gorra

safety helmet
el casco de seguridad

safety glasses
los lentes de seguridad

uniform
el uniforme

boots
las botas

gloves
los guantes

Danger!	**¡Peligro!**	Pay attention.	**Presta atención.**
Warning!	**¡Aviso!**	Be careful.	**Ten cuidado.**
Attention!	**¡Atención!**	Drive slowly.	**Maneja despacio.**
Hot!	**¡Caliente!**	Seek shelter.	**Busca refugio.**
Burns!	**¡Quema!**	Don't touch the blades.	**No toques las navajas.**
		wear	**usa**
		wash	**lava**

GRAMMAR

You recently learned that in Spanish we use the definite article "the" (el, la, los, las) when referring to parts of the body. It is also used with clothing items.

MATCHING EXERCISE

Write the letter of the picture next to the Spanish word it matches.

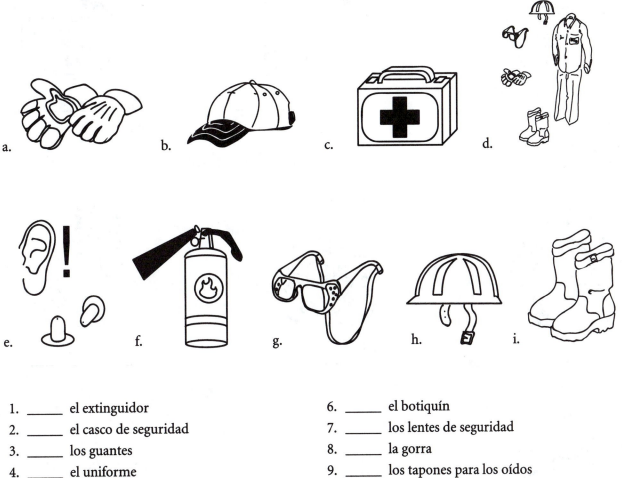

a. b. c. d.

e. f. g. h. i.

1. _____ el extinguidor
2. _____ el casco de seguridad
3. _____ los guantes
4. _____ el uniforme
5. _____ las botas

6. _____ el botiquín
7. _____ los lentes de seguridad
8. _____ la gorra
9. _____ los tapones para los oídos

VOCABULARY EXERCISE

Write the Spanish word for each picture in the space provided.

1. _____

2. _____

3. _____

4. _____

5. _____

6. _____

7. _____

8. _____

9. _____

MATCHING EXERCISE

Write the letter of the Spanish word next to the English word it matches on the left.

1. _____ uniform
2. _____ baseball cap
3. _____ gloves
4. _____ safety glasses
5. _____ safety helmet
6. _____ boots
7. _____ earplugs
8. _____ fire extinguisher
9. _____ first aid kit

a. el extinguidor
b. los tapones para los oídos
c. el uniforme
d. el botiquín
e. los lentes de seguridad
f. los guantes
g. el casco de seguridad
h. las botas
i. la gorra

CROSSWORD PUZZLES

Across

2. boots
4. gloves
7. first aid kit
9. safety helmet

Down

1. uniform
3. ear plugs
5. fire extinguisher
6. safety glasses
8. baseball cap

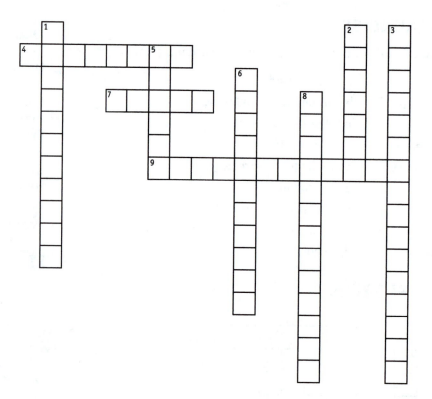

Across

4. tapones para los oídos
7. botas
9. casco de seguridad

Down

1. gorra
2. uniforme
3. extinguidor
5. guantes
6. botiquín
8. lentes de seguridad

TRANSLATION EXERCISE

Translate the following to English:

1. el botiquín _____
2. los guantes _____
3. casco de seguridad _____
4. el uniforme _____
5. la gorra _____
6. los lentes de seguridad _____
7. los tapones para los oídos _____
8. las botas _____
9. el extinguidor _____

Translate the following to Spanish:

1. first aid kit _____
2. fire extinguisher _____
3. baseball cap _____
4. boots _____
5. gloves _____
6. earplugs _____
7. safety glasses _____
8. safety helmet _____
9. uniform _____

MULTIPLE CHOICE

Circle the letter of the correct answer.

1. **safety helmet**
   a. los guantes
   b. los tapones para los oídos
   c. el casco de seguridad
   d. los lentes de seguridad

2. **boots**
   a. las botas
   b. los guantes
   c. la gorra
   d. el uniforme

3. **fire extinguisher**
   a. los lentes de seguridad
   b. el extinguidor
   c. el casco de seguridad
   d. el botiquín

4. **gloves**
   a. las botas
   b. el uniforme
   c. la gorra
   d. los guantes

5. **safety glasses**
   a. los guantes
   b. las botas
   c. el casco de seguridad
   d. los lentes de seguridad

6. **baseball cap**
   a. las botas
   b. la gorra
   c. el uniforme
   d. los guantes

7. **First Aid kit**
   a. el botiquín
   b. los lentes de seguridad
   c. el extinguidor
   d. el casco

8. **earplugs**
   a. el casco de seguridad
   b. los lentes de seguridad
   c. los tapones para los oídos
   d. los guantes

MATCHING EXERCISE

Write the letter of the Spanish word next to the English word it matches on the left.

1. _____ Be careful.
2. _____ Danger!
3. _____ Pay attention.
4. _____ Warning!
5. _____ Drive slowly.
6. _____ Hot!
7. _____ Seek shelter.
8. _____ Burns!
9. _____ Don't touch the blades.

a. ¡Aviso!
b. ¡Quema!
c. Busca refugio.
d. ¡Caliente!
e. No toques las navajas.
f. Ten cuidado.
g. Presta atención.
h. ¡Peligro!
i. Maneja despacio.

CROSSWORD PUZZLES

Across

4. Burns!
6. Drive slowly!
8. Seek shelter!

Down

1. Danger!
2. Hot!
3. Pay attention!
5. Be careful!
7. Attention!
9. Warning!

Across

5. ¡Peligro!
6. ¡Caliente!
7. ¡Ten cuidado!
8. ¡Aviso!

Down

1. ¡Busque refugio!
2. ¡Quema!
3. ¡Atención!
4. ¡Presta atención!
5. ¡Maneja despacio!

TRANSLATION EXERCISE

Translate the following to Spanish:

1. Drive slowly. _____

2. Pay attention. _____

3. Burns! _____

4. Hot! _____

5. Be careful. _____

6. Don't touch the blades. _____

7. Warning! _____

8. Danger! _____

9. Seek shelter. _____

Translate the following to English:

1. ¡Quema! _____

2. Busca refugio. _____

3. ¡Peligro! _____

4. Ten cuidado. _____

5. ¡Caliente! _____

6. No toques las navajas. _____

7. ¡Aviso! _____

8. Maneja despacio. _____

9. Presta atención. _____

MULTIPLE CHOICE

Circle the letter of the correct answer.

1. **Danger!**
   a. ¡Quema!
   b. ¡Peligro!
   c. ¡Aviso!
   d. ¡Caliente!

2. **Warning!**
   a. ¡Quema!
   b. ¡Peligro!
   c. ¡Aviso!
   d. ¡Caliente!

3. **Hot!**
   a. ¡Quema!
   b. ¡Peligro!
   c. ¡Aviso!
   d. ¡Caliente!

4. **Burns!**
   a. ¡Quema!
   b. ¡Peligro!
   c. ¡Aviso!
   d. ¡Caliente!

5. **Be careful.**
   a. Busca refugio.
   b. Ten cuidado.
   c. Presta atención.
   d. Maneja despacio.

6. **Pay attention.**
   a. Busca refugio.
   b. No toques las navajas.
   c. Presta atención.
   d. Maneja despacio.

7. **Drive slowly.**
   a. Maneja despacio.
   b. Busca refugio.
   c. Ten cuidado.
   d. No toques las navajas.

8. **Don't touch the blades.**
   a. Presta atención.
   b. Busca refugio.
   c. Ten cuidado.
   d. No toques las navajas.

REVIEW

Translate the following to Spanish:

1. What hurts? _____

2. My ankle hurts. _____

3. My back hurts. _____

4. Does your stomach hurt? _____

5. Wear the safety helmet and ear plugs. _____

6. Wear the uniform and baseball cap. _____

7. Wash the uniform. _____

8. Wear the gloves and boots. _____

9. Be careful! _____

10. Drive slowly! _____

11. Seek shelter! _____

12. Pay attention! _____

13. Don't touch the blades! _____

14. Danger! _____

15. Hot! _____

Read the dialogue aloud with a partner and then translate it to English.

Jill: ¿No te gusta estar con la familia?

Mark: Sí, pero* es sábado . . . juego béisbol a las tres.

Jill: ¿ Y el domingo? ¿Juegas golf?

Mark: Sí. Juego a las ocho.

Jill: No eres muy cooperativo. Es importante, Mark.

Mark: ¿Estás de mal humor, Jill?

Jill: Sí . . . ¡Estoy enojada y triste!

Mark: ¿Dónde está mi uniforme, gorra y guante?

Jill: No eres muy organizado, Mark.

Mark: ¿Qué hora es?

Jill: Son las dos y media.

Mark: Hasta luego.

Jill: ¡Maneja despacio!

Read the dialogue aloud with a partner and then translate it to Spanish.

Jill: Don't you like to be with the family?

Mark: Yes . . . but* it's Saturday . . . I play baseball at 3:00.

Jill: And Sunday? You play golf?

Mark: Yes. I play at 8:00.

Jill: You are not very cooperative. It's important, Mark.

Mark: Are you in a bad mood, Jill?

Jill: Yes . . . I am angry and sad!

Mark: Where is my uniform, hat and glove?

Jill: You are not very organized, Mark.

Mark: What time is it?

Jill: It's 2:30.

Mark: See you later.

Jill: Drive slowly!

(en el campo de béisbol)	(in the baseball field)
Jim: ¡Presta atención!	**Jim:** Pay attention!
Mark: Ten cuidado!	**Mark:** Be careful!
(dos jugadores chocan)	(two players collide)
Jim: ¡Ay! . . . no estoy bien. Estoy mal.	**Jim:** Aye . . . I'm not well. I'm bad.
Mark: ¿Qué te duele?	**Mark:** What hurts?
Jim: Me duele el brazo.	**Jim:** My arm hurts.
Mark: ¿Te duele el codo o la mano?	**Mark:** Does your elbow or hand hurt?
Jim: La mano.	**Jim:** My hand.
Mark: ¿Los dedos o el pulgar?	**Mark:** Your fingers or your thumb?
Jim: El pulgar. Mark . . . ¿Qué te duele?	**Jim:** My thumb. Mark . . . What hurts?
Mark: La pierna.	**Mark:** My leg.
Jim: ¿Te duele el tobillo o la rodilla?	**Jim:** Does your ankle or your knee hurt?
Mark: La rodilla.	**Mark:** My knee.
Jim: La rodilla está mal.	**Jim:** The knee is bad.
Mark: Estoy furioso. No puedo** jugar golf el domingo.	**Mark:** I'm furious. I can't** play golf on Sunday.
Jim: Puedes*** estar con la familia . . . puedes mirar la televisión y jugar cartas.	**Jim:** You can*** be with your family . . . you can watch television and play cards.
Mark: Sí . . . sí . . . ¿Dónde está el botiquín?	**Mark:** Yes . . . yes . . . Where is the first aid kit?
*pero – [but] **No puedo – I can't ***Puedes – you can	*but – pero **I can't – No puedo ***you can – Puedes

Translate the following to Spanish:

1. What's your name? _____

2. Where are you from? _____

3. Come with me. _____

4. Do it like me. _____

5. You're a hard worker! _____

6. Magnificent! _____

7. Where is? _____

8. How many? _____

9. When? _____

10. Monday, Tuesday, Wednesday _____

11. The woman is furious! _____

12. The foreman is worried and nervous. _____

13. I'm in a good mood! _____

14. Do you like to play billiards and bowl? _____

15. Do you like to play cards and go to parties? _____

16. I listen to music and I dance. _____

CULTURE: COMMUNICATION STYLES

In the Latino culture, as in many other cultures, saving face is important. All answers are given in order to avoid hurt feelings. As a result of this, evasive or half answers and "white lies" are common responses. These answers can be very confusing and problematic to a United States supervisor who has been raised to be open, direct, and above all, honest, in workplace situations.

In Latino cultures, yes may mean yes, maybe or even no. Latinos do not always say what they mean or mean precisely what they say. Latinos tend to hint, suggest or recommend rather than come out and say what they think. One can't always tell it like it is and be so blunt; that may upset the other person.

Maintaining harmony and saving face are key issues in the Latino society. The truth, if it disrupts harmony or a person may lose face, should be modified. Often a Latino tells his supervisor what he thinks his supervisor wants to hear. It's not always appropriate to disagree, or challenge (that disrupts harmony) or say no to co-workers. Protecting and reinforcing the personal relationship and bond is the goal of the communication process.

In the United States, yes means yes and no means no. Supervisors say what they mean and mean what they say. One does not need to read into what is said. In the United States it's important to "tell it like it is." Supervisors are less likely to imply and tend to state specifically what they think. A Latino woman interested in the communication field considers people in the United States blunt.

In the United States, telling the truth is valued more highly than sparing a person's feelings. The phrase "Honesty is the best policy" is so common in the United States society that it was the easiest $100 question on the television show, *Who Wants to be a Millionaire*! Giving and receiving information efficiently is the main goal of the communication process. It's okay in the United States to disagree and to challenge your boss or co-workers.

If a Latino makes a mistake, it is important for them to understand that if they admit the truth, they do not lose face with their supervisor. More likely, they will lose that respect if they don't admit a mistake and the mistake is found out later.

In order to get at the truth, it is important to have a good, trusting relationship with your Latino co-workers. A United States supervisor must be aware that a Latino will not open up to people with whom they are not close. Once that bond exists, supervisors find that their Latino co-workers become more open and direct with their answers.

7

Tools and Equipment Terms and Actions

PART I   TOOLS AND EQUIPMENT TERMS

blower
la sopladora

broom
la escoba

push broom
el cepillo

gas chainsaw
el serrucho de gas

pruner
la podadera

hose
la manguera

  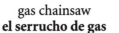

leaf rake
el rastrillo de hojas

soil rake
el rastrillo de tierra

pitchfork
la horca

rototiller
el rototiller

shovel
la pala

sledgehammer
el marro, el mazo

pick
el pico

    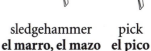

lawnmower
la máquina

wheelbarrow
la carretilla

tires
las llantas

oil
el aceite

gas
la gasolina

MATCHING EXERCISE

Write the letter of each picture next to the Spanish word it matches below.

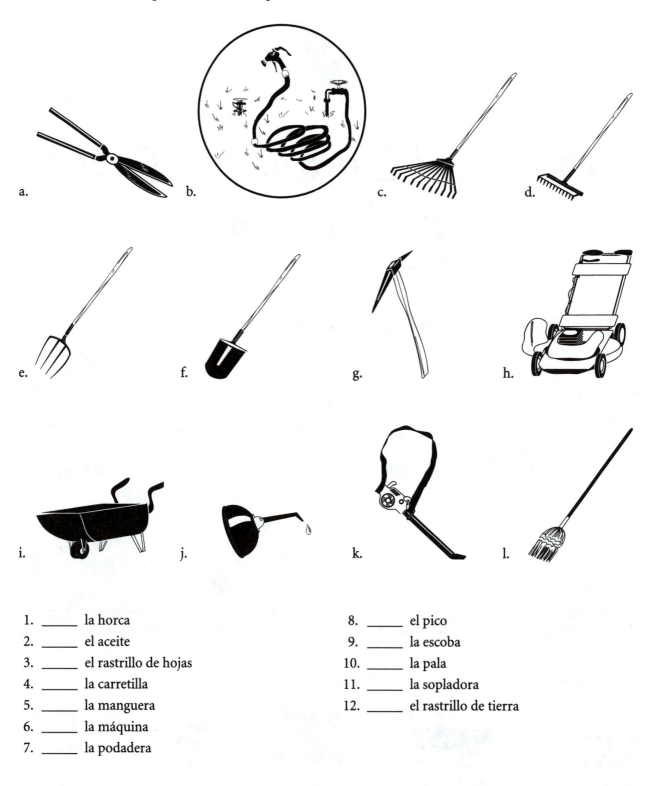

1. _____ la horca
2. _____ el aceite
3. _____ el rastrillo de hojas
4. _____ la carretilla
5. _____ la manguera
6. _____ la máquina
7. _____ la podadera

8. _____ el pico
9. _____ la escoba
10. _____ la pala
11. _____ la sopladora
12. _____ el rastrillo de tierra

VOCABULARY EXERCISE

Write the Spanish word for each picture in the space provided.

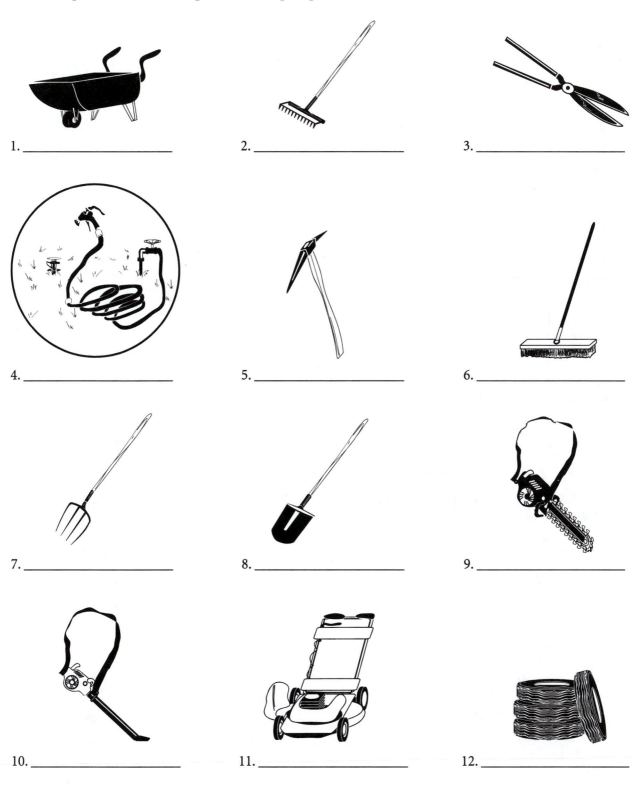

1. _____

2. _____

3. _____

4. _____

5. _____

6. _____

7. _____

8. _____

9. _____

10. _____

11. _____

12. _____

MATCHING EXERCISE

Write the letter of the Spanish word next to the English word it matches on the left.

1. _____ blower
2. _____ broom
3. _____ gas chainsaw
4. _____ pruner
5. _____ hose
6. _____ rake
7. _____ pitchfork
8. _____ rototiller
9. _____ shovel
10. _____ sledgehammer
11. _____ pick
12. _____ lawnmower
13. _____ wheelbarrow
14. _____ tires
15. _____ oil
16. _____ gas

a. la horca
b. el aceite
c. la gasolina
d. las llantas
e. el rototiller
f. la carretilla
g. la sopladora
h. la manguera
i. el marro, el mazo
j. la pala
k. el rastrillo
l. la podadera
m. el pico
n. la máquina
o. la escoba
p. el serrucho de gas

CROSSWORD PUZZLES

Across

1. wheelbarrow
8. blower
10. sledgehammer
12. pitch fork
13. gasoline
15. pruner

Down

2. soil rake
3. tires
4. broom
5. leaf rake
6. hose
7. lawnmower
9. pick
11. shovel
14. brush
16. oil

Across

1. carretilla
4. llantas
5. rastrillo de tierra
7. horca
8. mazo
9. podadera
10. gasolina
12. escoba
14. pala
15. máquina

Down

2. sopladora
3. pico
6. rastrillo de hojas
9. cepillo
11. manguera
13. aceite

TRANSLATION EXERCISE

Translate the following to English:

1. la sopladora _____
2. el aceite _____
3. la gasolina _____
4. la manguera _____
5. el rototiller _____
6. la carretilla _____
7. la horca _____
8. las llantas _____
9. el marro, el mazo _____
10. el serrucho de gas _____
11. el rastrillo _____
12. el pico _____
13. la podadera _____
14. la escoba _____
15. el cepillo _____
16. la pala _____

Translate the following to Spanish:

1. pruner _____
2. hose _____
3. rake _____
4. pitchfork _____
5. rototiller _____
6. blower _____
7. broom _____
8. push broom _____
9. gas chainsaw _____
10. lawnmower _____
11. wheelbarrow _____
12. shovel _____
13. sledgehammer _____
14. pick _____
15. tires _____
16. oil _____
17. gas _____

MULTIPLE CHOICE

Circle the letter of the correct answer.

1. **pruner**
   a. el rastrillo
   b. el pico
   c. la podadera
   d. el aceite

2. **hose**
   a. la sopladora
   b. el aceite
   c. gasolina
   d. la manguera

3. **wheelbarrow**
   a. la carretilla
   b. la horca
   c. las llantas
   d. el marro, el mazo

4. **blower**
   a. la sopladora
   b. la podadera
   c. la serrucho de gas
   d. el marro, el mazo

5. **broom**
   a. el rastrillo
   b. el pico
   c. la podadera
   d. la escoba

6. **rake**
   a. el rastrillo
   b. el pico
   c. la podadera
   d. la sopladora

7. **oil**
   a. la sopladora
   b. el aceite
   c. la gasolina
   d. la manguera

8. **pitchfork**
   a. la horca
   b. el pico
   c. la pala
   d. la escoba

GRAMMAR

Give me . . .   **Dame . . .**
                      Dame la escoba.

Give it to me:

Dámelo. (if the item ends in-o)
Dámela. (if the item ends in-a)

Don't worry too much about if the word ends in –o or –a. Your Latino co-worker will understand what you mean if you use *Dámelo* all the time.

ROLE PLAY

Many green industry organizations number their equipment. Ask your partner to give you an item. Follow the model.

ESTUDIANTE A:	Dame el pico.
ESTUDIANTE B:	¿Cinco?
ESTUDIANTE A:	Sí. Dámelo. Gracias.

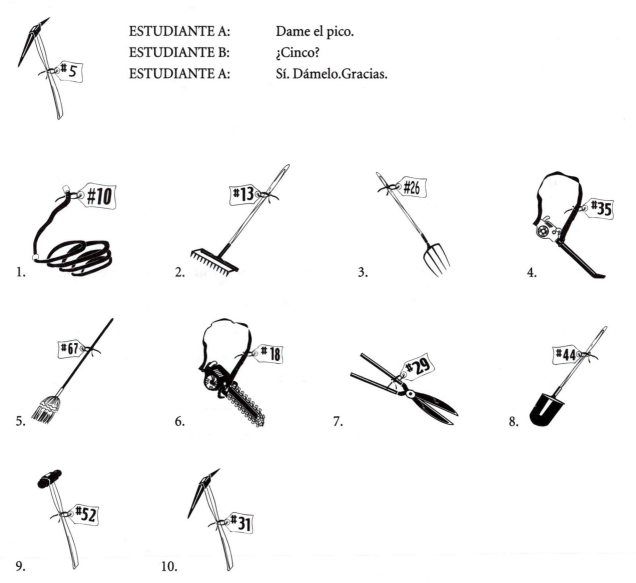

1.   2.   3.   4.

5.   6.   7.   8.

9.   10.

PART II   TOOLS AND EQUIPMENT ACTIONS

Group 1

wash	**lava**
put away	**guarda**
use	**usa**
load	**carga**
unload	**descarga**
mix	**mezcla**

Group 2

give me	**dame**
give him	**dale**
put	**pon**
clean	**limpia**
bring	**trae**
get	**consigue**
It doesn't work.	**No sirve.**
It's broken.	**Está roto, -a.**

GROUP 1

Matching Exercise

Write the letter of the Spanish word next to the English word it matches on the left.

1. _____ wash   a. descarga
2. _____ use   b. mezcla
3. _____ load   c. lava
4. _____ put away   d. guarda
5. _____ unload   e. carga
6. _____ mix   f. usa

Translate the following to English:

1. carga _____

2. mezcla _____

3. usa _____

4. descarga _____

5. lava _____

6. guarda _____

Translate the following to Spanish:

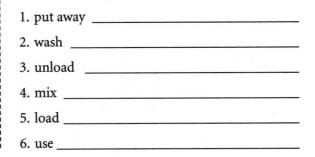

1. put away _____

2. wash _____

3. unload _____

4. mix _____

5. load _____

6. use _____

GROUP 2

Matching Exercise

Write the letter of the Spanish word next to the English word it matches on the left.

1. _____ get   a. trae
2. _____ give me   b. pon
3. _____ clean   c. dale
4. _____ put   d. consigue
5. _____ give him   e. limpia
6. _____ bring   f. dame

Translate the following to English:

1. consigue _____
2. limpia _____
3. dame _____
4. dale _____
5. trae _____
6. pon _____

Translate the following to Spanish:

1. bring _____
2. get _____
3. give me _____
4. give him _____
5. put _____
6. clean _____

MATCHING EXERCISE

Write the letter of the Spanish word next to the English word it matches on the left.

1. _____ wash   a. carga
2. _____ bring   b. regresa
3. _____ load   c. descarga
4. _____ use   d. usa
5. _____ unload   e. trae
6. _____ return   f. limpia
7. _____ put away   g. lava
8. _____ give me   h. consigue
9. _____ get   i. dame
10. _____ clean   j. guarda
11. _____ give him   k. mezcla
12. _____ mix   l. dale

CROSSWORD PUZZLES

Across

2. unload
6. bring
7. clean
8. load

Down

1. use
3. get
4. put away
5. give me

TEAM BUILDING TIP

It appears, nationwide, that there is a relationship/ communication gap between Latino workers and many Anglo equipment technicians. Latinos have said that they are afraid they will be yelled at by the technician for breaking the equipment. They try and fix the equipment by themselves or worse yet, don't turn it in at all. Several ideas to help this problem: (1) have better equipment training at the start of each season; (2) make it safe to tell the truth; (3) number and assign the equipment to each crew; (4) using masking tape, outline an area where workers can drop off broken tools, and (5) assign a buffer person between the technician and worker to handle broken equipment.

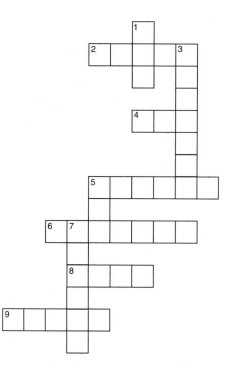

Across

2. trae
4. usa
5. dame
6. guarda
8. carga
9. limpia

Down

1. mezcla
3. dale
5. consigue
7. descarga

TRANSLATION EXERCISE

Translate the following to English:

1. lava _____
2. usa _____
3. regresa _____
4. guarda _____
5. carga _____
6. limpia _____
7. descarga _____
8. trae _____
9. consigue _____
10. dame _____
11. dale _____
12. mezcla _____

Translate the following to Spanish:

1. load _____
2. unload _____
3. bring _____
4. wash _____
5. use _____
6. put away _____
7. clean _____
8. give me _____
9. get _____
10. return _____
11. give him _____
12. mix _____

REVIEW

Translate the following to English:

1. Lava la carretilla. _____

2. Usa la sopladora. _____

3. Regresa el mazo. _____

4. Guarda el rastrillo. _____

5. Carga la manguera. _____

6. Lava las palas. _____

7. Descarga la máquina. _____

8. Trae el serrucho de gas. _____

9. Consigue el pico. _____

10. Dame la pala. _____

11. Mezcla el aceite y la gasolina. _____

12. Dale el cepillo. _____

Translate the following to Spanish:

1. Load the lawnmower. _____

2. Unload the wheelbarrow. _____

3. Bring the hose. _____

4. Wash the shovel. _____

5. Use the pick. _____

6. Put away the rake. _____

7. Mix the oil and gas. _____

8. Give me the gas chainsaw. _____

9. Get the pruner. _____

10. Use the broom. _____

11. Use the push broom. _____

12. Give him the blower. _____

Read the dialogue aloud with a partner and then translate it to English.

Frank: Ven conmigo.

Domingo: (Sigue a Frank al garaje)

Frank: Ayudame.

Domingo: Sí. ¡Eres el jefe!

Frank: Carga las sopladoras.

Domingo: ¿Y los rastrillos?

Frank: Sí. Carga las palas y los cepillos.

Domingo: ¿Y las máquinas?

Frank: Sí . . . mezcla el aceite y la gasolina.

Domingo: Okay.

Frank: Ay . . . y las podaderas. Gracias.
(más tarde en el sitio)

Domingo: ¿Descargo las máquinas?

Frank: Sí . . . Mírame. (arranca la máquina . . .)

Domingo: Buen trabajo.

Read the dialogue aloud with a partner and then translate it to Spanish.

Frank: Come with me.

Domingo: (follows Frank to the garage)

Frank: Help me.

Domingo: Yes. You're the boss!

Frank: Load the blowers.

Domingo: And the rakes?

Frank: Yes. Load the shovels and the brushes.

Domingo: And the lawnmowers?

Frank: Yes . . . mix the oil and the gas.

Domingo: Okay.

Frank: Oh . . . and the pruners. Thank you.
(later at the site)

Domingo: Unload the lawnmowers?

Frank: Yes . . . Watch me. (starts the lawn mower . . .)

Domingo: Good work.

Frank: Gracias. Hazlo como yo.

Domingo: Estoy nervioso . . . ¡Ay!

Frank: ¿Estás bien? Te duele el pie?

Domingo: No . . . no . . . estoy bien.

Frank: Por favor . . . ¡No toques las navajas!

Domingo: Okay. (Mira el pie . . . sube la máquina.)

Frank: Domingo . . . Trátalo.

Domingo: ¿Está bien?

Frank: Continua tratando, Domingo.

Domingo: ¿Está correcto?

Frank: Sí. Excelente!

Domingo: (Maneja muy mal.)

Frank: ¡Maneja despacio!

Domingo: ¡AYÚDAME!

Frank: Thank you. Do it like me.

Domingo: I'm nervous . . . Aye!

Frank: Are you okay? Does your foot hurt?

Domingo: No . . . no . . . I'm bad.

Frank: Please . . . Don't touch the blades!

Domingo: Okay. (Looks at his foot . . . gets on the mower.)

Frank: Domingo . . . Try it.

Domingo: Is it good?

Frank: Keep trying, Domingo.

Domingo: Is it correct?

Frank: Yes. Excellent!

Domingo: (Drives off recklessly.)

Frank: Drive slowly!

Domingo: HELP ME!

Translate the following to Spanish:

1. Hello. Welcome. _____

2. I'd like to introduce you to . . . _____

3. Nice to meet you. Same to you. _____

4. Watch me. Do it like me. _____

5. Try it. Continue trying. _____

6. You're a hard worker! _____

7. Thursday Friday Saturday _____

8. February March November _____

9. There is a party. How many pizzas? _____

10. I play golf. Do you like to play golf? _____

11. The crew is hardworking! _____

12. My brother is the foreman. _____

13. Does your ankle hurt? _____

14. There is blood. _____

15. Where is the first aid kit? _____

CULTURE: TRAINING

Effective training is one of the most crucial and important matters in any organization. In Latin American countries it is highly theoretical, and there are few structured programs. In the United States, however, training is concrete, specific and very practical. Structured training programs are widely used in successful companies.

When training, an issue to consider is an employee's attitude toward uncertainty. It varies in different cultures. In the United States, people do not fear taking a risk or failing. When asked to volunteer in front of a group, many often do. Trial and error is how they learn and improve their skills, products and services.

In many Latin cultures, taking a risk and failing in front of others is to be avoided if at all possible. Ask for a volunteer from a group of Latinos, and the vast majority of heads look down. One doesn't try something new unless he knows it works. He/She may feel very unsure of his/her abilities. If they fail, they may not try again. For the most part, Latinos are receptive and eager to learn new methods and appreciate the opportunity for training very much. They can, however, become discouraged if they feel that they are being told the only way to do a task is the "American way."

When training and developing an unsure employee in any culture, it is important to build his/her self esteem. Praise the employee every small step of the way so that they become more self confident in their abilities. They will perform the task better if they are not nervous about making a mistake.

8

Grounds Maintenance Terms and Actions

PART I   GROUNDS MAINTENANCE TERMS

shrubs
los arbustos

branches
las ramas

clippings
el cortado

flowers
las flores

grass
el zacate, el pasto

hole
el hoyo

leaves
las hojas

plants
las plantas

roots
las raíces

seeds
las semillas

soil
la tierra

trees
los árboles

weeds
las hierbas

MATCHING EXERCISE

Write the letter of each picture next to the Spanish word it matches below.

a. b. c. d.

e. f. g. h.

i. j. k. l.

1. _____ el hoyo
2. _____ las plantas
3. _____ el zacate, el pasto
4. _____ las raíces
5. _____ las hierbas
6. _____ las flores

7. _____ las ramas
8. _____ la tierra
9. _____ las hojas
10. _____ las semillas
11. _____ los árboles
12. _____ los arbustos

VOCABULARY EXERCISE

Write the Spanish word for each picture in the space provided.

1. _____

2. _____

3. _____

4. _____

5. _____

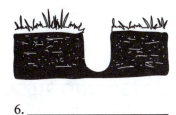

6. _____

7. _____

8. _____

9. _____

10. _____

11. _____

12. _____

MATCHING EXERCISE

Write the letter of the Spanish word next to the English word it matches on the left.

1. _____ flowers   a. tierra
2. _____ weeds   b. hierbas
3. _____ soil   c. arbustos
4. _____ shrubs   d. plantas
5. _____ grass   e. semillas
6. _____ plants   f. raíces
7. _____ leaves   g. flores
8. _____ seeds   h. ramas
9. _____ branches   i. hojas
10. _____ clippings   j. pasto, zacate
11. _____ roots   k. árboles
12. _____ trees   l. el cortado

CROSSWORD PUZZLES

Across

1. shrubs
3. roots
5. branches
10. trees
11. plant
12. leaves

Down

2. soil
4. grass
6. seeds
7. weeds
8. flowers
9. hole

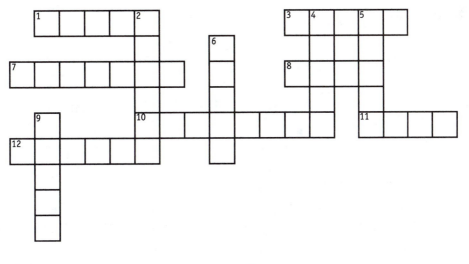

Across

1. árboles
3. zacate
7. flores
8. hoyo
10. ramas
11. tierra
12. hojas

Down

2. arbustos
4. raíces
5. semillas
6. planta
9. hierbas

TRANSLATION EXERCISE

Translate the following to English:

1. los árboles _____
2. las hojas _____
3. el pasto, el zacate _____
4. las ramas _____
5. los arbustos _____
6. las raíces _____
7. el cortado _____
8. las flores _____
9. el hoyo _____
10. las plantas _____
11. la tierra _____
12. las hierbas _____

Translate the following to Spanish:

1. trees _____
2. leaves _____
3. shrubs _____
4. flowers _____
5. seeds _____
6. branches _____
7. weeds _____
8. grass _____
9. clippings _____
10. plants _____
11. soil _____
12. roots _____

MULTIPLE CHOICE

Circle the letter of the correct answer.

1. **shrubs**
   a. árboles
   b. hoyo
   c. arbustos
   d. hierbas

2. **branches**
   a. ramas
   b. hoyo
   c. hojas
   d. raíces

3. **clippings**
   a. flores
   b. plantas
   c. cortado
   d. zacate

4. **flowers**
   a. flores
   b. plantas
   c. cortado
   d. zacate

5. **hole**
   a. árboles
   b. hoyo
   c. arbustos
   d. hierbas

6. **branches**
   a. ramas
   b. hoyo
   c. hojas
   d. raíces

7. **trees**
   a. árboles
   b. hoyo
   c. arbustos
   d. hierbas

8. **leaves**
   a. ramas
   b. hoyo
   c. hojas
   d. raíces

9. **seeds**
   a. semillas
   b. raíces
   c. tierra
   d. zacate

10. **weeds**
    a. plantas
    b. hoyo
    c. arbustos
    d. hierbas

11. **roots**
    a. ramas
    b. hoyo
    c. hojas
    d. raíces

12. **soil**
    a. semillas
    b. raíces
    c. tierra
    d. zacate

PART II GROUNDS MAINTENANCE ACTIONS

Group 1		Group 2	
blow	**sopla**	prune	**poda**
dig	**excava**	rake	**rastrilla**
plant	**planta**	prepare	**prepara**
take out	**saca**	spray	**rocía**
install	**instala**	get	**consigue**
water	**riega**	mulch	**muele**

GROUP 1

Matching Exercise

Write the letter of the Spanish word next to the English word it matches on the left.

1. _____ water   a. planta
2. _____ dig   b. instala
3. _____ plant   c. riega
4. _____ take out   d. sopla
5. _____ blow   e. excava
6. _____ install   f. saca

Translate the following to English:	*Translate the following to Spanish:*
1. instala _____	1. water _____
2. saca _____	2. plant _____
3. planta _____	3. dig _____
4. riega _____	4. install _____
5. sopla _____	5. take out _____
6. excava _____	6. blow _____

GROUP 2

Matching Exercise

Write the letter of the Spanish word next to the English word it matches on the left.

1. _____ prune   a. rocía
2. _____ rake   b. consigue
3. _____ prepare   c. muele
4. _____ get   d. poda
5. _____ spray   e. rastrilla
6. _____ mulch   f. prepara

Translate the following to English:	*Translate the following to Spanish:*
1. consigue _____	1. mulch _____
2. poda _____	2. prune _____
3. rastrilla _____	3. prepare _____
4. muele _____	4. rake _____
5. rocía _____	5. get _____
6. prepara _____	6. spray _____

CROSSWORD PUZZLES

Across

3. prune
6. get
7. plant
8. blow
9. water
10. mulch
11. dig

Down

1. spray
2. rake
3. prepare
4. take out
5. install

Across

2. excava
5. rocía
6. planta
7. consigue
8. sopla
10. saca
11. poda

Down

1. prepara
3. instala
4. rastrilla
9. riega

REVIEW

Translate the following to English:

1. Riega las flores. _____
2. Prepara la tierra. _____
3. Sopla el cortado. _____
4. Rastrilla las hojas. _____
5. Planta las flores. _____
6. Instala los árboles. _____
7. Muele las plantas. _____
8. Saca las hierbas. _____
9. Poda las ramas. _____
10. Excava el hoyo. _____
11. Consigue las flores. _____
12. Rocía el zacate. _____

Translate the following to Spanish:

1. Get the plants. _____
2. Dig the hole. _____
3. Take out the weeds. _____
4. Mulch the plants. _____
5. Prune the branches. _____
6. Water the shrubs. _____
7. Get the soil. _____
8. Rake the leaves. _____
9. Blow the clippings. _____
10. Prepare the soil. _____
11. Prune the trees. _____
12. Spray the grass. _____

GRAMMAR: FOLLOWING UP ON JOB ASSIGNMENTS

You have learned several commands to assign morning tasks. If you want to follow up with a worker later that afternoon to see if they have completed the assignment, you use the past tense.

The –a ending changes to the –aste ending and you raise your voice in a questioning tone. Spanish does not have the words "Did you." They are implied in the –aste ending. Read the Spanish words aloud and practice raising your voice.

| Plant . . . | Planta . . . |
| Did you plant. . . ? | ¿Plantaste. . . ? |

| Blow . . | Sopla . . . |
| Did you blow . . . | ¿Soplaste . . . |

| Prune . . . | Poda . . . |
| Did you prune . . . | ¿Podaste. . . |

The –e ending changes to the –iste ending.

| Get . . . | Consigue . . . |
| Did you get . . . | ¿Conseguiste. . . ? |

| Mulch . . . | Muele . . . |
| Did you mulch . . . | ¿Moliste*. . . ? |

*This form is irregular

ROLE PLAY

Did you...? It's the end of the day and you and your employee are driving back to the office. Ask and answer if certain tasks have been done. Follow the model.

ESTUDIANTE A:	¿Podaste los arbustos?
ESTUDIANTE B:	Sí.
	No, todavia, no. (No, not yet.)

prune

1. plant

2. blow

3. get

4. prune

5. dig

6. pull

7. rake

8. spray

TRANSLATION EXERCISE

Translate the following to English:

1. ¿Preparaste. . . ? _____

2. ¿Podaste. . . ? _____

3. ¿Plantaste. . . ? _____

4. ¿Sacaste. . . ? _____

5. ¿Instalaste. . . ? _____

6. ¿Rociaste. . . ? _____

7. ¿Conseguiste. . . ? _____

8. ¿Moliste. . . ? _____

Translate the following to Spanish:

1. Did you plant the flowers? _____

2. Did you blow the leaves? _____

3. Did you dig the hole? _____

4. Did you install the trees? _____

5. Did you prune the branches? _____

6. Did you take out the weeds? _____

7. Did you spray the weeds? _____

8. Did you rake the leaves? _____

Read the dialogue aloud with a partner and then translate it to English.

Jack: Hola Miguel. ¿Qué tal?

Miguel: ¡Buenos días, jefe!

Jack: Quiero presentarte a Alejandro.

Miguel: Mucho gusto.

Alejandro: Igualmente.

Miguel: ¿De dónde eres, Alejandro?

Alejandro: Soy de Aguascalientes, México.

Miguel: Soy de Guatemala. Soy guatamalteco.

Jack: Miguel . . . vete a los apartamentos.

Miguel: Está bién.

Read the dialogue aloud with a partner and then translate it to Spanish.

Jack: Hello Miguel. How's it going?

Miguel: Good morning, boss!

Jack: I'd like to introduce you to Alejandro.

Miguel: Nice to meet you.

Alejandro: Same to you.

Miguel: From where are you, Alejandro?

Alejandro: I'm from Aguascalientes, Mexico.

Miguel: I'm from Guatemala. I'm Guatemalan.

Jack: Miguel . . . go to the apartments.

Miguel: Okay.

Jack: Planta los árboles.	**Jack:** Plant the trees.
Miguel: ¿Y las flores?	**Miguel:** And the flowers?
Jack: Sí. Riega los árboles y las flores.	**Jack:** Yes. Water the trees and the flowers.
Miguel: ¿Y corta el zacate?	**Miguel:** And cut the grass?
Jack: Sí . . . y por favor . . . saca las hierbas.	**Jack:** Yes . . . and please . . . take out the weeds.
Miguel: Saca las raíces . . . sí, sí . . .	**Miguel:** Pull the roots . . . yes, yes. . .
Jack: Gracias. ¡Eres muy trabajador!	**Jack:** Thank you. You're a hard worker!
(por la tarde)	(later that afternoon)
Jack: ¿Qué tal, Miguel?	**Jack:** How's it going, Miguel?
Miguel: Bien . . . perfecto.	**Miguel:** Fine . . . perfect.
Jack: ¿Hay problemas?	**Jack:** Are there problems?
Miguel: Ah . . . Estoy preocupado.	**Miguel:** Ah . . . I am worried.
Jack: ¿Por qué?	**Jack:** Why?
Miguel: Ah . . . ¡La mujer está furiosa!	**Miguel:** Ah . . . The woman is furious!
Jack: ¿Por qué?	**Jack:** Why?
Jack: ¿Plantaste los árboles?	**Jack:** Did you plant the trees?
Miguel: Sí, jefe. Y las flores.	**Miguel:** Yes, boss. And the flowers.
Jack: ¿Podaste los arbustos?	**Jack:** Did you prune the shrubs?
Miguel: Sí, señor.	**Miguel:** Yes, sir.
Jack: Hmmm . . .	**Jack:** Hmmm . . .
Miguel: Ven conmigo, Jack. Hay mucha agua . . .	**Miguel:** Come with me, Jack. There is a lot of water . . .
Jack: Oh, no! ¡Sí . . . La mujer está de mal humor!	**Jack:** Oh, no! ¡Yes . . . The woman is in a bad mood!

Translate the following to Spanish:

1. I'm studying Spanish. _____

2. Do you speak English? _____

3. It's good. It's bad. It's correct. _____

4. Everything else is perfect. _____

5. Incredible! You're very strong! _____

6. Who is the manager? _____

7. Where is the foreman? _____

8. There are seven days in a month. _____

9. I like the summer. I swim. I fish. _____

10. Do you swim? Do you fish? _____

11. Does your ankle hurt? _____

12. Where is the first aid kit? _____

13. Give me the pruner. _____

14. Load the blowers. _____

15. Mix the oil and gas. _____

CULTURE: HOW A COUNTRY'S HISTORY AFFECTS BEHAVIOR

There are so many differences between the United States and Latin American countries in their values, behavior, and lifestyles. These differences affect how business is conducted. A comparison of their histories helps to explain why the cultures are so different today.

Every high school student in the United States took the class "United States History." To pass exams, they memorized the dates of battles *won*, territory *added* to the nation or some other *positive* accomplishment. During the middle 1800s, Mexico wouldn't sell their land to the United States, so they fought for it. Popular historic sayings were "The West was won!" and "The Making of America!" To this day, United States citizens give little thought to anything being lost.

As a result of their past, United States citizens are considered positive, optimistic, self-confident, and able leaders. They don't fear a challenge. They are adventurers who are willing to take a risk. They want to change things, improve them, make them better, quicker, stronger and safer. They are forward thinkers.

The Mexican story was different. They are a conquered people. In the 1500s, Cortez and his small band of soldiers completed the Conquest in less than two years and extended Spanish dominion south into Central America and as far north as Alaska. Spain ruled Mexico for the next three hundred years. In the 1800s, Maximillian and the French ruled. Then in 1846, the Mexican American war took place and Mexico lost more than half of their territory to a self-confident United States. It was a monumental event and a devastating loss of face.

This continuous presence of a dominant group made some Latino cultures feel that if you were white, you were superior. It created a sense of inferiority. Some Latinos feel that the Spanish conquerors deliberately created an oppressed underclass with a mentality rooted in passivity and underachievement. The concept of authority has become the norm.

In the United States, "All men are created equal." In Latin American countries, differences make a difference. It is a very hierarchical society. Age, sex, role and rank are extremely important.

TEAM BUILDING TIP

In order for Spanish-speaking employees to keep current with the news in their countries, it would be good to order them a subscription to their country's daily newspaper. The Mexican newspaper, *La Prensa,* can be found at www.laprensa.com

9

Materials and Containers

PART I   MATERIALS TERMS

fertilizer
el fertilizante

peat moss
la turba

soil
la tierra

bark
la corteza

pine straw
la paja

mulch (mixture)
la mezcla

sand
la arena

compost
el abono

seeds
las semillas

bricks
los ladrillos

stones
las piedras

rock
la roca

sod
el zacate

cement
el cemento

clay
el barro

MATCHING EXERCISE

Write the letter of the picture next to the Spanish word it matches.

a.

b.

c.

d.

e.

f.

g.

h.

i.

j.

k.

l.

1. _____ la tierra

2. _____ la corteza

3. _____ la paja

4. _____ la mezcla

5. _____ el fertilizante

6. _____ la turba

7. _____ las semillas

8. _____ la arena

9. _____ el abono

10. _____ las piedras

11. _____ la roca

12. _____ los ladrillos

VOCABULARY EXERCISE

Write the Spanish word for each picture in the space provided

1. _____   2. _____   3. _____   4. _____

      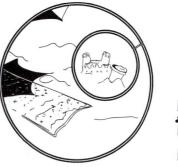   

5. _____   6. _____   7. _____   8. _____

9. _____   10. _____   11. _____   12. _____

MATCHING EXERCISE

Write the letter of the Spanish word next to the English word it matches on the left.

1. _____ sand
2. _____ compost
3. _____ seeds
4. _____ bricks
5. _____ fertilizer
6. _____ peat moss
7. _____ soil
8. _____ bark

9. _____ pine straw
10. _____ mulch
11. _____ sod
12. _____ cement
13. _____ clay
14. _____ stones
15. _____ rock

a. la mezcla
b. la paja
c. la roca
d. la tierra
e. el fertilizante
f. la turba
g. el zacate
h. la corteza

i. el cemento
j. la arena
k. el abono
l. las semillas
m. el barro
n. las piedras
o. los ladrillos

CROSSWORD PUZZLES

Across

1. rock
5. mixture
6. bark
7. soil
8. sod
11. compost
12. bricks
13. fertilizer
15. clay

Down

2. sand
3. seeds
4. pine straw
9. cement
10. stones
14. peat moss

Across

1. roca
5. turba
7. paja
8. mezcla
9. zacate
11. ladrillos
15. tierra

Down

2. abono
3. fertilizante
4. arena
6. semillas
10. corteza
12. cemento
13. piedras
14. barro

TRANSLATION EXERCISE

Translate the following to English:

1. los ladrillos _____

2. las piedras _____

3. la roca _____

4. la paja _____

5. la mezcla _____

6. la arena _____

7. el abono _____

8. las semillas _____

9. el zacate _____

10. el cemento _____

11. el barro _____

12. el fertilizante _____

13. la turba _____

14. la tierra _____

15. la corteza _____

Translate the following to Spanish:

1. seeds _____

2. bricks _____

3. fertilizer _____

4. peat moss _____

5. pine straw _____

6. mulch _____

7. sand _____

8. soil _____

9. bark _____

10. compost _____

11. stones _____

12. cement _____

13. clay _____

14. rock _____

15. sod _____

MULTIPLE CHOICE

Circle the letter of the correct answer.

1. sand
   a. la turba
   b. la tierra
   c. la corteza
   d. la arena

2. compost
   a. el abono
   b. el fertilizante
   c. la arena
   d. el zacate

3. seeds
   a. las piedras
   b. las semillas
   c. los ladrillos
   d. la mezcla

4. stones
   a. las piedras
   b. las semillas
   c. los ladrillos
   d. la mezcla

5. rock
   a. la paja
   b. la roca
   c. la corteza
   d. la turba

6. sod
   a. la turba
   b. los ladrillos
   c. la tierra
   d. el zacate

7. bricks
   a. el cemento
   b. las piedras
   c. las semillas
   d. los ladrillos

8. peat moss
   a. la paja
   b. la roca
   c. la corteza
   d. la turba

9. soil
   a. la tierra
   b. la arena
   c. el barro
   d. la turba

10. bark
  a. la paja
  b. la roca
  c. la corteza
  d. la turba

11. pine straw
  a. la paja
  b. la roca
  c. la corteza
  d. la turba

12. mulch
  a. el abono
  b. la fertilizante
  c. el zacate
  d. la mezcla

PART II CONTAINER TERMS

Containers

bag	**el saco**
pallet	**la paleta**
pot (plastic, clay)	**la maceta (de plástico, de barro)**
can	**la lata**
pile	**el montón**
box	**la caja**
wheelbarrow	**la carretilla**
car trunk	**el baúl**

Sizes

1 inch	**una pulgada**
2 inches	**dos pulgadas**
1 foot	**un pie**
2 feet	**dos pies**
2 by 3	**dos por tres**
1/2 yard	**media yarda**
1 yard	**una yarda**
2 yards	**dos yardas**
1 gallon	**un galón**
2 gallons	**dos galones**
3 gallons	**tres galones**
5 gallons	**cinco galones**
15 gallons	**quince galones**
25 gallons	**veinte cinco galones**

TEAM BUILDING TIP

Have a coat drive at your company—better yet, have a warm clothes drive. In many regions of the United States it is still very cold in March, April, and May, and your employees may not own good, warm winter coats, hats, and gloves.

MATCHING EXERCISE

Write the letter of the Spanish word next to the English word it matches on the left.

1. _____ pot
2. _____ bag
3. _____ car trunk
4. _____ inches
5. _____ feet
6. _____ gallons

7. _____ pallet
8. _____ pile
9. _____ box
10. _____ wheelbarrow
11. _____ can
12. _____ yards

a. la lata
b. las yardas
c. la carretilla
d. la maceta
e. los galones
f. las pulgadas

g. los pies
h. la caja
i. el montón
j. el baúl
k. la paleta
l. el saco

CROSSWORD PUZZLES

Across

3. gallons
4. pallet
6. can
7. car trunk
8. bag
9. feet
10. wheelbarrow

Down

1. yards
2. box
4. inches
5. pot

Across

4. montón
5. pies
7. baúl
8. caja
9. galones

Down

1. pulgadas
2. carretilla
3. paleta
4. maceta
6. lata
8. saco

TRANSLATION EXERCISE

Translate the following to English:

1. pulgadas _____
2. pies _____
3. la carretilla _____
4. los galones _____
5. la paleta _____
6. el montón _____
7. la maceta _____
8. el saco _____
9. el baúl _____
10. la lata _____
11. las yardas _____
12. la caja _____

Translate the following to Spanish:

1. pot _____
2. bag _____
3. car trunk _____
4. inches _____
5. feet _____
6. gallons _____
7. pallet _____
8. pile _____
9. box _____
10. wheelbarrow _____
11. can _____
12. yards _____

MULTIPLE CHOICE

Circle the letter of the correct answer.

1. **pot**
   a. la paleta
   b. la lata
   c. la maceta
   d. la caja

2. **bag**
   a. el saco
   b. el baúl
   c. la carretilla
   d. el montón

3. **inches**
   a. las yardas
   b. las pulgadas
   c. los galones
   d. los pies

4. **car trunk**
   a. el saco
   b. el baúl
   c. la carretilla
   d. el montón

5. **feet**
   a. las yardas
   b. las pulgadas
   c. los galones
   d. los pies

6. **gallons**
   a. las yardas
   b. las pulgadas
   c. los galones
   d. los pies

7. **pallet**
   a. la paleta
   b. la lata
   c. la maceta
   d. la caja

8. **pile**
   a. el saco
   b. el baúl
   c. la carretilla
   d. el montón

9. **box**
   a. la paleta
   b. la lata
   c. la maceta
   d. la caja

10. **wheelbarrow**
    a. el saco
    b. el baúl
    c. la carretilla
    d. el montón

11. **can**
    a. la paleta
    b. la lata
    c. la maceta
    d. la caja

12. **yards**
    a. las yardas
    b. las pulgadas
    c. los galones
    d. los pies

PART III   ACTIONS TO USE WITH MATERIALS

Group 1		*Group 2*	
apply	**aplica**	add	**añade**
rake	**rastrilla**	sweep	**barre**
load	**carga**	get	**consigue**
unload	**descarga**	brush	**cepilla**
take out	**saca**	tamp	**pisa**
spread	**empareja**	put	**pon**

GROUP 1

Matching Exercise

Write the letter of the Spanish word next to the English word it matches on the left.

1. _____ unload   a. carga
2. _____ take out   b. saca
3. _____ spread   c. empareja
4. _____ apply   d. rastrilla
5. _____ rake   e. descarga
6. _____ load   f. aplica

Translate the following to English:

1. empareja _____
2. aplica _____
3. rastrilla _____
4. carga _____
5. saca _____
6. descarga _____

Translate the following to Spanish:

1. rake _____
2. apply _____
3. unload _____
4. take out _____
5. spread _____
6. load _____

GROUP 2

Matching Exercise

Write the letter of the Spanish word next to the English word it matches on the left.

1. _____ get   4. _____ add
2. _____ brush   5. _____ sweep
3. _____ tamp   6. _____ put

a. pon   d. cepilla
b. añade   e. pisa
c. barre   f. consigue

Translate the following to English:

1. pisa _____
2. pon _____
3. añade _____
4. barre _____
5. consigue _____
6. cepilla _____

Translate the following to Spanish:

1. put _____
2. add _____
3. get _____
4. brush _____
5. tamp _____
6. sweep _____

CROSSWORD PUZZLES

Across

1. put
2. load
4. take out
6. sweep
7. brush
9. spread
10. apply
11. get

Down

1. tamp
3. rake
5. add
8. unload

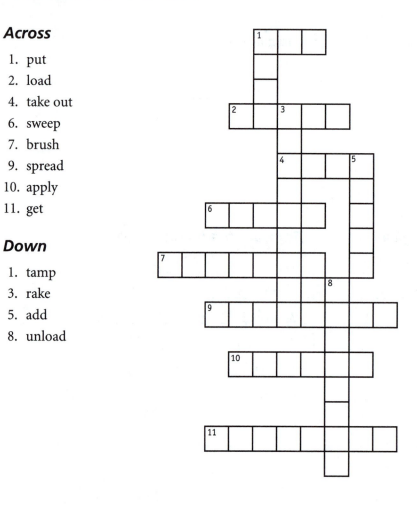

Across

3. pon
4. carga
5. consigue
7. aplica
8. añade
10. descarga
11. pisa

Down

1. empareja
2. rastrilla
6. saca
9. cepilla

Role Play

What's Miguel doing? Work with a partner. Ask and answer. ¿Qué hace Miguel? Follow the model.

ESTUDIANTE A:	¿Que hace Miguel?
ESTUDIANTE B:	Miguel carga la tierra.

carga

1. rastrilla

2. empareja

3. añade

4. barre

5. carga

6. descarga

7. saca

8. spread

GRAMMAR: HE AND SHE

He   **él**

She   **ella**

In the past several chapters you have learned to assign tasks by using the command form. You have learned to speak directly to a person. Now, using the same form of the verb, you can speak about a person. Study the following examples.

Talking directly to a person:
Hi, Raul! Please . . . plant the flowers. Thanks.   **Hola, Raúl! Por favor . . . planta las flores. Gracias.**

Talking about a person:
Raul plants the flowers.   **Raúl planta las flores.**

Translate the following to English:

1. Pepe, carga la tierra, por favor. _____

2. Juan carga la tierra. _____

3. Ana, aplica el fertilizante, por favor. _____

4. Teresa aplica el fertilizante. _____

REVIEW

Translate the following to English:

1. Paco, carga las piedras, por favor. _____

2. José carga las piedras. _____

3. Rosa, pisa la tierra, por favor. _____

4. Ana pisa la tierra. _____

5. Alberto, descarga los ladrillos, por favor. _____

6. Javier descarga los ladrillos. _____

7. Maria, get the peat moss. _____

8. Antonio takes out the clay. _____

9. Paco, añade más mezcla, por favor. _____

10. Jesús rastrilla la arena. _____

Translate the following to Spanish:

1. Paco, please, load the stones. _____

2. Javier loads the stones. _____

3. Juan, please, get the fertilizer. _____

4. Carlos gets the fertilizer. _____

5. Pilar, spread out the soil, please. _____

6. Teresa spreads out the soil. _____

7. Arturo, add more mulch, please. _____

8. Ana, get the pine straw, please. _____

9. Susana spreads the pine straw. _____

10. Jesús gets the peat moss. _____

Read the story aloud and then translate it to English.

Jim es el jefe de la compañía Green Landscapes, Inc. Jim trabaja mucho en los meses de marzo, abril, mayo, junio y julio. Jim es muy responsable. Jim trabaja mucho en la oficina y con los clientes. Es el gerente de la región.

    Jack trabaja mucho. Jack supervisa muchos Latinos—tres cuadrillas. Jack estudia español y su profesora es muy paciente y organizada. Se llama Kathy. Jack practica el español mucho con Kathy y con las cuadrillas.

    Los Latinos son muy cooperativos y trabajadores.

    Miguel es de Guadalajara, México. Miguel es el mayordomo de la cuadrilla. Tiene 32 años. Domingo, Paco y Berto son hermanos. Miguel es su tío. Domingo corta el zacate. Domingo saca las hierbas y las raíces. Paco sopla las hojas mientras* Berto rastrilla las hojas. Domingo poda los arbustos. Miguel planta y riega las flores.

    Por la tarde**, Jack estudia mucho el vocabulario en español. Jack practica con Miguel. Jack y Miguel saben que*** la comunicación es igual a la productividad.

    *mientras – while
     **Por la tarde – In the afternoon
    ***saben que – know that
****es igual a – is equal to, equals

Read the story aloud and then translate it to Spanish.

Jim is the boss of the Green Landscapes Company, Inc. Jim works a lot in the months of March, April, May, June and July. Jim is very responsible. Jim works a lot in the office and with the clients. Jim is the manager of the region.

    Jack works a lot. Jack supervises many Latinos—three crews. Jack studies Spanish and his professor is very patient and organized. Her name is Kathy. Jack practices Spanish a lot with Kathy and the crews.

    The Latinos are very cooperative and hard working.

    Miguel is from Guadalajara, Mexico. Miguel is the foreman of the crew. He is thirty two years old. Domingo, Paco and Berto are brothers. Miguel is their uncle. Domingo cuts the grass. Domingo takes out the weeds and pulls the roots. Paco blows the leaves while* Berto rakes the leaves. Domingo prunes the shrubs. Miguel plants and waters the flowers.

    In the afternoon**, Jack studies the Spanish vocabulary a lot. Jack practices with Miguel. Jack and Miguel know that*** communication equals**** productivity.

    *while – mientras
     **In the afternoon – Por la tarde
    ***know that – saben que
****equal – es igual a

Translate the following to Spanish:

1. How's your family? _____

2. Carlos is from Honduras. He's Honduran. _____

3. Help me. Watch me. _____

4. Try it. Keep trying. _____

5. How many? When? Where? _____

6. What time is it? _____

7. I'm angry. I'm tired. I'm sick. _____

8. What's your wife's name? _____

9. What's your daughter's name? _____

10. How old is your son? _____

11. Do you like to play volleyball? _____

12. I like to play cards. Do you play cards? _____

13. Get the wheelbarrow. _____

14. Load the blowers and the rakes. _____

15. Wear the safety glasses, gloves, and boots. _____

CULTURE: DIRECTING AND SUPERVISING

One of the most significant and troublesome work-related issues involves how people treat their differences and how supervisors and subordinates interact with one another. Cultures differ in how they view a person's age, sex, role and rank. In the United States, there is a tendency to downplay such factors, but in Latin American cultures, these differences are important and very meaningful.

Latinos highly respect authority. Traditionally, young employees never doubt or even comment on a decision their superior has made, even if they completely disagree with it. Nor do supervisors ordinarily accept such questioning from subordinates. In Latin American countries, there is no custom of delegation of authority; the idea is foreign to most people. The supervisor keeps the power and concerns are decided at the top. Subordinates are not proactive, and they wait for specific instructions. Most subordinates like this approach better, since it frees them from making mistakes and from losing face. Many times subordinates feel insecure and fear making errors. It is important, though, to point out that a new generation of supervisors is growing up which, as a result of university training, firmly supports the custom of delegating responsibility.

In the United States, people are raised to be independent, and people like to make their own decisions. As a result, young employees are normally reluctant to ask for advice. They want as much responsibility and authority as is allowed. Having authority being exercised over them is distasteful, and they don't like having to ask for approval for every decision and action they take. They feel capable and want to be allowed to make the majority of decisions by themselves.

They thrive on tackling new problems by themselves. They have a strong self-esteem in their judgements and are aware that a small mistake will not lose them the support and respect of their supervisors, because making a minor mistake at the start is regarded as normal in the learning process. A common phrase in the United States is we learn from our mistakes. Latinos should not feel uncomfortable admitting they made an error.

10

Nursery Terms and Actions

PART I   NURSERY TERMS

sun	shade
el sol	**la sombra**

tags, labels
las etiquetas

prices
los precios

names
los nombres

annuals
las anuales

perennials
las perennes

pallet
la paleta

hanging baskets
las canastas colgadas

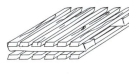

pot
la maceta

cart
el carrito

flat
el flat

container
el recipiente

potting bench
la mesa de plantar

MATCHING EXERCISE

Write the letter of each picture next to the Spanish word it matches below.

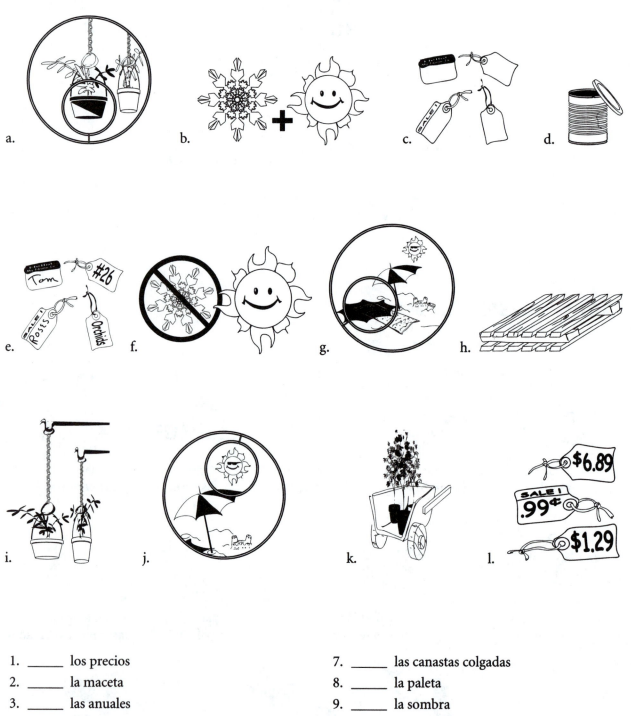

a.   b.   c.   d.

e.   f.   g.   h.

i.   j.   k.   l.

1. _____ los precios
2. _____ la maceta
3. _____ las anuales
4. _____ las perennes
5. _____ los nombres
6. _____ las etiquetas

7. _____ las canastas colgadas
8. _____ la paleta
9. _____ la sombra
10. _____ el recipiente
11. _____ el carrito
12. _____ el sol

VOCABULARY EXERCISE

Write the Spanish word for each picture in the space provided.

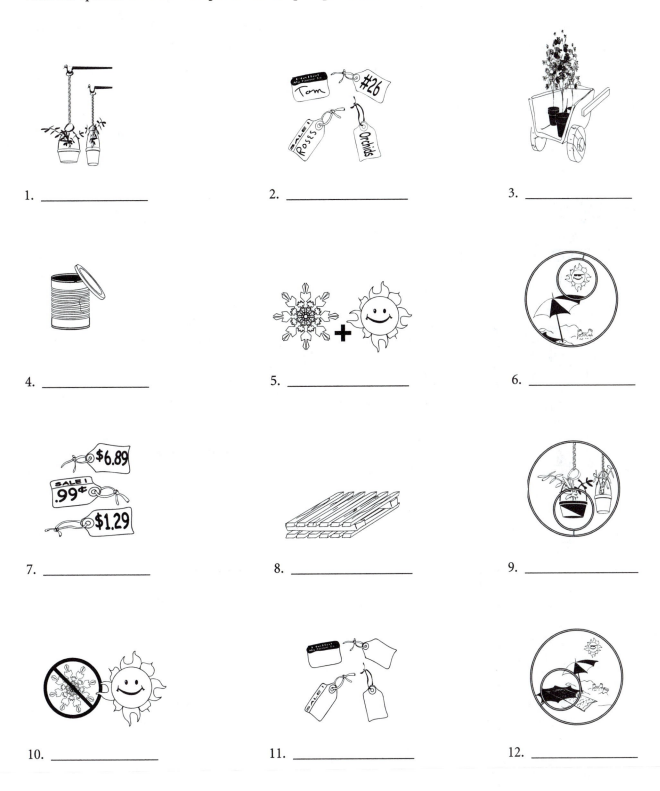

1. _____

2. _____

3. _____

4. _____

5. _____

6. _____

7. _____

8. _____

9. _____

10. _____

11. _____

12. _____

MATCHING EXERCISE

Write the letter of the Spanish word next to the English word it matches on the left.

1. _____ tags, labels
2. _____ prices
3. _____ names
4. _____ annuals
5. _____ perennials
6. _____ pallet
7. _____ hanging baskets
8. _____ pot

9. _____ cart
10. _____ flat
11. _____ container
12. _____ potting bench
13. _____ sun
14. _____ shade
15. _____ plants

a. el carrito
b. las perennes
c. la mesa de plantar
d. la sombra
e. los precios
f. el recipiente
g. la maceta

h. las canastas colgadas
i. el flat
j. las etiquetas
k. la paleta
l. las plantas
m. las anuales
n. el sol
o. los nombres

CROSSWORD PUZZLES

Across

1. prices
5. cart
6. pallet
8. names
9. shade
11. plants
12. perennials
14. flat
15. container

Down

2. tags, labels
3. sun
4. pot
7. annuals
10. hanging basket
13. potting bench

Across

4. plantas
8. carrito
9. flat
10. sombra
11. nombres
12. perennes
13. recipiente
14. maceta

Down

1. mesa de plantar
2. sol
3. anuales
4. precios
5. etiquetas
6. canastas colgadas
7. paleta

TRANSLATION EXERCISE

Translate the following to English:

1. el carrito _____

2. las perennes _____

3. la mesa de plantar _____

4. el sol _____

5. los precios _____

6. el recipiente _____

7. la maceta _____

8. las canastas colgadas _____

9. el flat _____

10. las etiquetas _____

11. la paleta _____

12. las plantas _____

13. las anuales _____

14. la sombra _____

15. los nombres _____

Translate the following to Spanish:

1. annuals _____

2. perennials _____

3. pallet _____

4. tags, labels _____

5. prices _____

6. names _____

7. hanging baskets _____

8. pot _____

9. shade _____

10. sun _____

11. plants _____

12. cart _____

13. flat _____

14. container _____

15. potting bench _____

MULTIPLE CHOICE

Circle the letter of the correct answer.

1. **potting bench**
   a. el carrito
   b. la maceta
   c. la mesa de plantar
   d. la sombra

2. **pallet**
   a. los precios
   b. la paleta
   c. la maceta
   d. las etiquetas

3. **prices**
   a. los precios
   b. la paleta
   c. las plantas
   d. las etiquetas

4. **shade**
   a. las anuales
   b. los precios
   c. la sombra
   d. las plantas

5. **cart**
   a. los perennes
   b. la mesa de plantar
   c. las macetas
   d. el carrito

6. **container**
   a. el recipiente
   b. la maceta
   c. el flat
   d. la paleta

7. **hanging baskets**
   a. las anuales
   b. los precios
   c. las canastas colgadas
   d. la mesa de plantar

8. **tags, labels**
   a. los precios
   b. los nombres
   c. las plantas
   d. las etiquetas

9. **pot**
   a. los precios
   b. la maceta
   c. la paleta
   d. el flat

10. **perennials**
    a. las perennes
    b. la paleta
    c. las plantas
    d. los precios

PART II NURSERY ACTIONS

Group 1		Group 2	
pot	**planta**	dig up	**saca**
repot	**replanta**	weed	**desherbar**
deadhead	**corta la mala**	put, tag	**pon**
prepare	**prepara**	ball	**haz bola**
move	**mueve**	burlap	**pon en costal**
get	**consigue**	load	**carga**
wrap	**envuelve**	unload	**descarga**

GROUP 1

Matching Exercise

Write the letter of the Spanish word next to the English word it matches on the left.

1. _____ deadhead   a. planta
2. _____ pot   b. envuelve
3. _____ prepare   c. consigue
4. _____ move   d. replanta
5. _____ repot   e. saca la mala
6. _____ get   f. prepara
7. _____ wrap   g. mueve

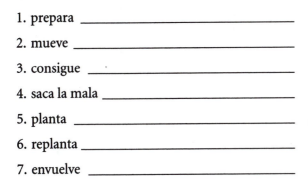

Translate the following to English:

1. prepara _____
2. mueve _____
3. consigue _____
4. saca la mala _____
5. planta _____
6. replanta _____
7. envuelve _____

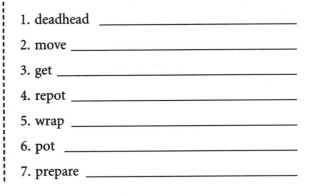

Translate the following to Spanish:

1. deadhead _____
2. move _____
3. get _____
4. repot _____
5. wrap _____
6. pot _____
7. prepare _____

GROUP 2

Matching Exercise

Write the letter of the Spanish word next to the English word it matches on the left.

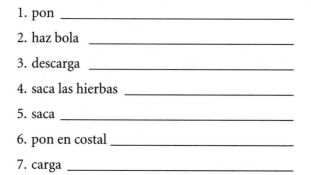

1. _____ dig up   a. descarga
2. _____ put, tag   b. carga
3. _____ unload   c. pon
4. _____ ball   d. saca las hierbas
5. _____ burlap   e. pon en costal
6. _____ load   f. saca
7. _____ weed   g. haz bola

Translate the following to English:

1. pon _____

2. haz bola _____

3. descarga _____

4. saca las hierbas _____

5. saca _____

6. pon en costal _____

7. carga _____

Translate the following to Spanish:

1. weed _____

2. ball _____

3. burlap _____

4. dig up _____

5. load _____

6. put, tag _____

7. unload _____

CROSSWORD PUZZLES

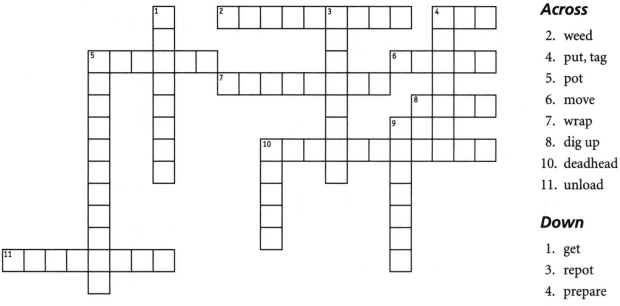

Across

2. weed
4. put, tag
5. pot
6. move
7. wrap
8. dig up
10. deadhead
11. unload

Down

1. get
3. repot
4. prepare
5. burlap
9. ball
10. load

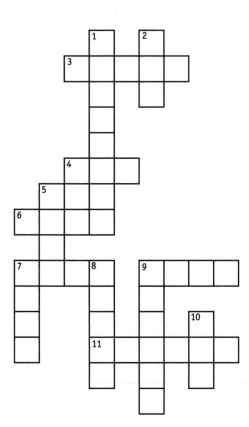

Across

3. replanta
4. consigue
6. carga
7. deshierba
9. haz bola
11. descarga

Down

1. corta la mala
2. planta
5. mueve
7. envuelve
8. saca
9. pon en costal
10. pon

MULTIPLE CHOICE

Circle the letter of the correct answer.

1. **move**
   a. carga
   b. saca
   c. mueve
   d. envuelve

2. **get**
   a. consigue
   b. carga
   c. mueve
   d. pon

3. **prepare**
   a. pon costal
   b. planta
   c. pon
   d. prepara

4. **wrap**
   a. mueve
   b. envuelve
   c. haz bola
   d. pon costal

5. **dig up**
   a. carga
   b. descarga
   c. saca
   d. saca las hierbas

6. **pot**
   a. replanta
   b. planta
   c. saca
   d. carga

7. **ball**
   a. haz bola
   b. saca las hierbas
   c. pon costal
   d. corta la mala

8. **burlap**
   a. prepara
   b. envuelve
   c. haz bola
   d. pon en costal

9. **load**
   a. mueve
   b. consigue
   c. descarga
   d. carga

10. **repot**
    a. replanta
    b. prepara
    c. pon
    d. planta

11. **deadhead**
    a. pon
    b. mueve
    c. saca las hierbas
    d. corta la mala

12. **weed**
    a. saca
    b. saca las hierbas
    c. corta la mala
    d. pon

13. **put, tag**
    a. saca
    b. carga
    c. planta
    d. pon

14. **unload**
    a. descarga
    b. saca
    c. carga
    d. mueve

ROLE PLAY

Tag the plants. Your nursery's getting ready for the new spring rush! Your co-worker asks what you want him to tag.... Pick and choose your response from the following materials. Follow the model.

ESTUDIANTE A:	¿Qué quieres?
ESTUDIANTE B:	Pon los precios en las plantas.

PART III   COLORS

red	**rojo**	orange	**anaranjado**
white	**blanco**	pink	**rosado**
blue	**azul**	black	**negro**
green	**verde**	brown	**café**
purple	**morado**	grey	**gris**
yellow	**amarillo**		

MATCHING EXERCISE

Write the letter of the Spanish word next to the English word it matches on the left.

1. _____ black   a. morado
2. _____ brown   b. negro
3. _____ red   c. café
4. _____ white   d. anaranjado
5. _____ green   e. verde
6. _____ blue   f. gris
7. _____ grey   g. azul
8. _____ pink   h. rosado
9. _____ orange   i. rojo
10. _____ yellow   j. blanco
11. _____ purple   k. amarillo

CROSSWORD PUZZLES

Across

3. yellow
4. brown
6. grey
8. black
9. white
10. purple

Down

1. green
2. pink
3. orange
5. blue
7. red

Across

2. morado
5. verde
6. amarillo
9. café
10. rojo

Down

1. azul
2. rosado
3. anaranjado
4. negro
7. blanco
8. gris

TRANSLATION EXERCISE

Translate the following to English:

1. verde _____
2. amarillo _____
3. rojo _____
4. blanco _____
5. azul _____
6. anaranjado _____
7. rosado _____
8. negro _____
9. morado _____
10. café _____
11. gris _____

Translate the following to Spanish:

1. blue _____
2. green _____
3. red _____
4. white _____
5. purple _____
6. grey _____
7. yellow _____
8. orange _____
9. black _____
10. brown _____
11. pink _____

MULTIPLE CHOICE

Circle the letter of the correct answer.

1. **pink**
   a. anaranjado
   b. rosado
   c. rojo
   d. morado

2. **green**
   a. gris
   b. azul
   c. verde
   d. blanco

3. **purple**
   a. anaranjado
   b. morado
   c. azul
   d. amarillo

4. **red**
   a. rosado
   b. blanco
   c. café
   d. rojo

5. **yellow**
   a. rojo
   b. verde
   c. anaranjado
   d. amarillo

6. **blue**
   a. morado
   b. gris
   c. azul
   d. verde

7. **white**
   a. blanco
   b. azul
   c. morado
   d. negro

8. **black**
   a. blanco
   b. azul
   c. morado
   d. negro

9. **orange**
   a. anaranjado
   b. rosado
   c. rojo
   d. morado

10. **brown**
    a. negro
    b. blanco
    c. gris
    d. café

GRAMMAR: DESCRIPTIVE WORDS

When describing items in Spanish, the descriptive word (the color, in this case) comes after the item. Study the examples.

| the red plants | las plantas rojas |
| the white shrubs | los arbustos blancos |

TRANSLATION EXERCISE

Translate the following to Spanish:

1. the orange pots _____

2. the pink tags _____

3. the white perennials _____

4. the red annuals _____

5. the blue flats _____

6. the brown containers _____

7. the purple plants _____

8. the green trees _____

9. the yellow shrubs _____

10. the red hanging baskets _____

GRAMMAR: EXPRESSING WANTS

To express wants and desires in Spanish we use the verb Querer. Study the examples.

Do you want . . .?	**¿Quieres . . .?**
What do you want?	**¿Qué quieres?**
I want	**Quiero**

ROLE PLAY

You got the job! Pretend that you are a landscape architect and your design was chosen for the new development in town.

You are at the nursery buying your materials. Working with a partner, ask and answer what you want and how many you want. Follow the model.

ESTUDIANTE A:	¿Qué quiere, señor?
ESTUDIANTE B:	Quiero los arbustos rojos.
ESTUDIANTE A:	¿Cuántos?
ESTUDIANTE B:	Nueve.

1.

white, 5

2.

pink, 18

3.

orange, 13

4.

yellow, 10

5.

purple, 6

6.

brown, 12

7.

red, 16

8.

green, 14

9.

black, 15

10.

blue, 20

11.

red, 9

TRANSLATION EXERCISE

Translate the following to English:

1. ¿Qué quieres? _____

2. Quiero tres canastas colgadas rojas. _____

3. Quiero cinco macetas anaranjadas. _____

4. ¿Quieres las anuales blancas? _____

5. ¿Quieres las etiquetas rosadas? _____

6. ¿Qué quieres? _____

7. Quiero diez y seis flats amarillos. _____

8. Quiero doce plantas verdes. _____

9. ¿Quieres los flats azules? _____

10. ¿Quieres dos macetas moradas? _____

Translate the following to Spanish:

1. I want ten green pots. _____

2. I want five yellow flats. _____

3. Do you want the pink annuals? _____

4. Do you want the purple perennials? _____

5. What do you want? _____

6. I want twenty blue tags. _____

7. I want three orange pots. _____

8. Do you want the black containers? _____

9. Do you want the white hanging baskets? _____

10. What do you want? _____

REVIEW

Translate the following to English:

1. Envuelve las plantas rosadas. _____

2. Consigue las plantas. _____

3. ¿Qué quieres? Carga las paletas. _____

4. Replantar las anuales blancas. _____

5. Saca las hierbas en las canastas colgadas. _____

6. ¿Qué quieres? Pon los precios. _____

7. Consigue el carrito. _____

8. Envuelve las perennes moradas. _____

9. Mueve el recipiente negro. _____

10. Corta la mala de las plantas. _____

11. ¿Sol o sombra? _____

12. Prepara la mesa de plantar. _____

Translate the following to Spanish:

1. Tag the yellow annuals. _____

2. Move the hanging baskets. _____

3. Dig up the brown plants. _____

4. Put the plants in the sun. _____

5. Sun or shade? _____

6. What do you want? Get the orange pot. _____

7. Load the pallet. _____

8. Wrap the blue perennials. _____

9. What do you want? Tag the prices. _____

10. Repot the white plants. _____

11. Deadhead the annuals. _____

12. Put the plants in the shade. _____

Read the dialogue aloud with a partner and then translate it to English.

(en el club de tennis)

Sarah: ¿Quieres jugar más tenis, Judy?

Judy: No. Estoy cansada. ¿Quieres jugar el jueves?

Sarah: Sí. . .¿A qué hora?

Judy: ¿A las diez o diez y media?

Sarah: A las diez. ¿A dónde vas?

Judy: Voy a Tall Trees Nursery. ¡Es primavera!

(en Tall Trees Nursery)

Leo: ¡Bienvenidos a Tall Trees, Judy!

Judy: Gracias. Estoy nerviosa. ¡Es mi primer día!

Leo: ¿Hablas español, Judy?

Judy: Sí. . .un poco.

Read the dialogue aloud with a partner and then translate it to Spanish.

(in the tennis club)

Sarah: Do you want to play more tennis, Judy?

Judy: No. I'm tired. Do you want to play on Thursday?

Sarah: Yes . . . At what time?

Judy: At ten or ten thirty?

Sarah: At ten. Where are you going?

Judy: I'm going to Tall Trees Nursery. It's Spring!

(in Tall Trees Nursery)

Leo: Welcome to Tall Trees, Judy!

Judy: Thank you. I am nervous. It's my first day!

Leo: Do you speak Spanish, Judy?

Judy: Yes. . . a little.

Leo: Ven conmigo. . .

Judy: ¿Qué quieres?

Leo: Primero saca la mala de las perennes.

Judy: ¿Y saca las hierbas?

Leo: Sí. Replanta las anuales blancas.

Judy: ¿En macetas de plástico o barro?

Leo: De barro. Riega las canastas colgadas.

Judy: ¿Pon los precios y nombres?

Leo: Sí. Eres muy organizada, Judy.

Judy: Gracias.

Leo: ¡Eres muy trabajador!

Customer: Buenos días.

Judy: Hola. . .¿Qué quieres?

Customer: Quiero dos flats de anuales rojas.

Judy: ¿Qué más?

Customer: Dos flats de perennes rosadas.

Judy: ¿Quieres un carrito?

Customer: Sí. ¡Perfecto!

Judy: ¿Quieres un saco de turba?

Customer: Sí y un saco de mezcla y fertilizante.

Judy: ¿Quieres paja o abono?

Customer: No, gracias.

Judy: Muy bien. Es cuarenta dólores.

Customer: (trata de llevar todo)

Judy: Octavio, ayuda ala mujer, por favor.

Customer: Muchas gracias, Octavio. Adios.

Leo: Come with me. . .

Judy: What do you want?

Leo: First deadhead the perennials.

Judy: And take out the weeds?

Leo: Yes. Repot the white annuals.

Judy: In plastic or clay pots?

Leo: Clay. Water the hanging baskets.

Judy: Tag the prices and names?

Leo: Yes. You are very organized, Judy.

Judy: Thank you.

Leo: You're a hard worker!

Customer: Good morning.

Judy: Hello. What would you like?

Customer: I want two flats of red annuals.

Judy: What else?

Customer: Two flats of pink perennials.

Judy: Do you want a cart?

Customer: Yes. Perfect!

Judy: Do you want a bag of peat moss?

Customer: Yes and a bag of mulch and fertilizer.

Judy: Do you want pine straw or compost?

Customer: No, thank you.

Judy: Very good. It's forty dollars.

Customer: (attempts to carry it all)

Judy: Octavio, help the woman, please.

Customer: Thanks a lot, Octavio. Good bye.

Translate the following to Spanish:

1. Welcome! What's your name? _____

2. Nice to meet you. Same to you. _____

3. It's important. It's not correct. _____

4. Everything else is perfect! _____

5. Monday, Wednesday, Friday _____

6. Do you want to play cards? _____

7. Do you want to eat? _____

8. The crew is tired. Are you sick? _____

9. My uncle is the foreman. _____

10. Does your ankle hurt? _____

11. Where is the first aid kit? _____

12. Blow the leaves. Did you plant the shrubs? _____

13. There are five blowers and five rakes. _____

14. Wear the safety glasses and gloves. _____

15. The neighbor is worried and angry. _____

CULTURE: LEADERSHIP TIPS FOR LATINOS

As Anglo businesses grow, they are looking to Latino employees to take on positions of leadership. But what Anglos don't understand is that many Latinos tend to like the job that they currently have. Many Latinos will sacrifice riches for safety and security.

Working at Anglo businesses, Latinos are at a crossroads. They can either struggle on with a secure, yet low-paying job and muddle through *poco a poquito*, or they can recognize and seize a great opportunity. To be a successful Latino leader in the United States, in addition to learning about the two cultures, you need to:

1. Study the culture sections in this textbook.

Good business depends on effective communication, so it is important for Latinos dealing with Anglo businesses to speak the same language. Most Anglos speak only English. Even though they are hiring Spanish-speaking employees, they feel they shouldn't have to learn Spanish. If a Latino wants to be successful working in the United States, it is essential to learn English. It is the most fundamental business skill.

2. Learn English.

3. Trust others.

This is the most controversial characteristic with Latinos. Before trusting others, many Latinos feel that you should first study people, check them out thoroughly. They feel it is better to be safe than sorry. At first, this seems reasonable, but ultimately it is not. Lack of trust and overcaution breeds more of the same to the point that everyone is distrustful. If a person feels he is honest and trustworthy, others will feel that way about him or her as well. Trust breeds trust and distrust breeds distrust. This is a positive attitude to live by.

4. Change your "Don't make waves" attitude.

Latinos are hesitant to state their opinions. Anglos, on the other hand, can't wait to give their opinions. Opinions and ideas are the basis of business success. The Anglos value the Latinos' opinions very much yet Latino employees remain silent. Since many Latinos are working in the trenches they know a lot of information (i.e., what works and doesn't work). Latinos must believe in themselves and give their valuable input. Learning to be more open and free with feelings, opinions and intimacies will also help build a trusting, long-lasting relationship.

5.   Always do what you say you will do.

To be successful in business, as well as in life, remember the letters: DWYSYWD. Backwards or forwards it stands for "Do what you say you will do." Or in Spanish, *Dicho y hecho:* "Once spoken, it's done." Make sure to keep every promise you make. Perhaps it is stereotypical, but to a large degree, it is a Latino's nature to feel okay if they don't quite keep a commitment. Perhaps it is a Latino's reluctance to say "no." If you cannot do what you said you would or something goes wrong, tell your boss or client as soon as you know it yourself. It happens to everybody. Very often they will help you with the problem.

Are Latin immigrants destined to become an entrenched underclass? Will they always be the "working poor"? Latinos must understand their mind set and once aware of it, they can change. Latinos are the bridge between the Americas. Companies would be crazy not to hire and promote Latinos—and they know it. They need you. They are making it easy for you. Now you must recognize certain factors within yourself that may be obstacles to your success. Once you are aware of them you can overcome them. Believe in yourself. You have a lot to offer. It's a great time to be a bilingual, bicultural Latino in the United States.

Commercial and Residential Sites

PART I COMMERCIAL SITE TERMS

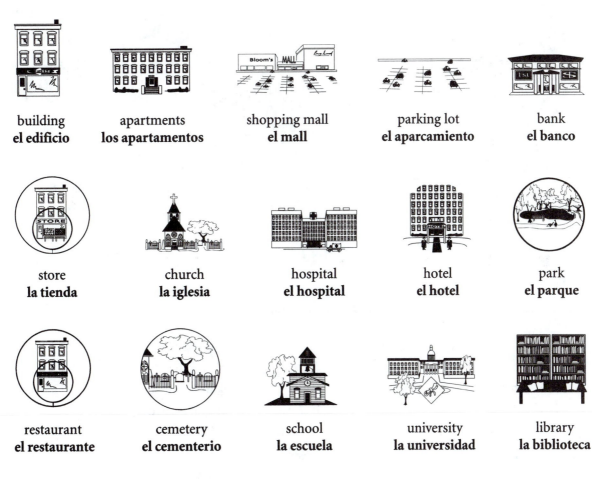

building
el edificio

apartments
los apartamentos

shopping mall
el mall

parking lot
el aparcamiento

bank
el banco

store
la tienda

church
la iglesia

hospital
el hospital

hotel
el hotel

park
el parque

restaurant
el restaurante

cemetery
el cementerio

school
la escuela

university
la universidad

library
la biblioteca

MATCHING EXERCISE

Write the letter of the picture next to the Spanish word it matches.

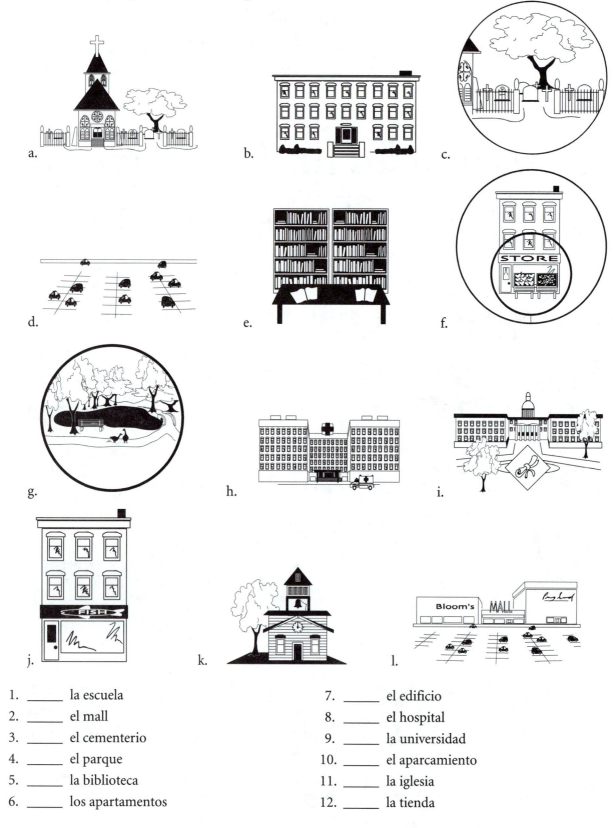

a.
b.
c.
d.
e.
f.
g.
h.
i.
j.
k.
l.

1. _____ la escuela
2. _____ el mall
3. _____ el cementerio
4. _____ el parque
5. _____ la biblioteca
6. _____ los apartamentos

7. _____ el edificio
8. _____ el hospital
9. _____ la universidad
10. _____ el aparcamiento
11. _____ la iglesia
12. _____ la tienda

VOCABULARY EXERCISE

Write the Spanish word for each picture in the space provided.

1. _____

2. _____

3. _____

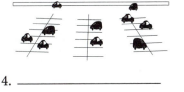

4. _____

5. _____

6. _____

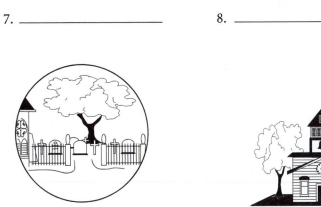

7. _____

8. _____

9. _____

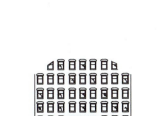

10. _____

11. _____

12. _____

MATCHING EXERCISE

Write the letter of the Spanish word next to the English word it matches on the left.

1. _____ bank
2. _____ church
3. _____ hospital
4. _____ building
5. _____ apartments
6. _____ shopping mall
7. _____ store
8. _____ parking lot

9. _____ hotel
10. _____ park
11. _____ restaurant
12. _____ library
13. _____ cemetery
14. _____ school
15. _____ university

a. la iglesia
b. la biblioteca
c. el cementerio
d. el hotel
e. la escuela
f. el hospital
g. la tienda
h. el restaurante

i. el edificio
j. el parque
k. el banco
l. el aparcamiento
m. los apartamentos
n. la universidad
o. el mall

CROSSWORD PUZZLES

Across

4. church
5. parking lot
6. apartments
9. university
11. mall
13. hospital
15. school

Down

1. cemetery
2. store
3. bank
7. restaurant
8. library
10. building
12. hotel
14. park

Across

3. universidad
7. tienda
9. hospital
11. restaurante
12. biblioteca
13. aparcamiento
14. banco
15. escuela

Down

1. cementerio
2. edificio
4. mall
5. apartamentos
6. iglesia
8. hotel
10. parque

TRANSLATION EXERCISE

Translate the following to English:

1. la tienda _____

2. el edificio _____

3. el parque _____

4. el banco _____

5. el cementerio _____

6. el hotel _____

7. el aparcamiento _____

8. la escuela _____

9. el hospital _____

10. el restaurante _____

11. los apartamentos _____

12. la universidad _____

13. el mall _____

14. la iglesia _____

15. la biblioteca _____

Translate the following to Spanish:

1. park _____

2. restaurant _____

3. cemetery _____

4. church _____

5. university _____

6. school _____

7. bank _____

8. library _____

9. shopping mall _____

10. store _____

11. parking lot _____

12. hotel _____

13. hospital _____

14. building _____

15. apartments _____

MULTIPLE CHOICE

Circle the letter of the correct answer.

1. **school**
   a. la escuela
   b. el edificio
   c. el parque
   d. el banco

2. **church**
   a. la universidad
   b. el mall
   c. la iglesia
   d. la biblioteca

3. **park**
   a. el edificio
   b. el parque
   c. el banco
   d. el aparcamiento

4. **restaurant**
   a. el hotel
   b. la escuela
   c. el hospital
   d. el restaurante

5. **cemetery**
   a. el edificio
   b. el parque
   c. el banco
   d. el cementerio

6. **university**
   a. la escuela
   b. el edificio
   c. la universidad
   d. el hospital

7. **building**
   a. el edificio
   b. la escuela
   c. la biblioteca
   d. el aparcamiento

8. **store**
   a. la universidad
   b. escuela
   c. la tienda
   d. el edificio

9. **bank**
   a. la biblioteca
   b. el banco
   c. la iglesia
   d. la escuela

10. **apartments**
    a. el hotel
    b. el hospital
    c. el aparcamiento
    d. los apartamentos

GRAMMAR: "TO GO" AND "GOING"

> To Go: **Ir** (this verb is irregular)
>
> Where are you going?   **¿Adónde vas?**
>
> I'm going, I go   **Voy**
> We're going, We go   **Vamos**
> John's going, John goes **Va**

Translate the following to English:

1. Voy _____

2. Vamos _____

3. ¿Adónde vas? _____

4. Va _____

5. Voy _____

6. Vamos _____

Translate the following to Spanish:

1. Where are you going? _____

2. I'm going _____

3. Mary is going _____

4. We go _____

5. We're going _____

6. I go _____

EXPRESSING "GOING TO" WITH PLACES

To express "to the" there are four forms in Spanish. Study the following examples.

I'm going to the store.	Voy **a la** tienda.
I'm going to the offices.	Voy **a las** oficinas.
I'm going to the bank.	Voy **al** banco.
I'm going to the apartments.	Voy **a los** apartamentos.

ROLE PLAY

Where are you going? Imagine it is Saturday morning. Working with a partner, ask and answer where you are going during the weekend. Use the question ¿Adónde vas? Follow the model.

ESTUDIANTE A:	¿Adónde vas?
ESTUDIANTE B:	Voy a . . .

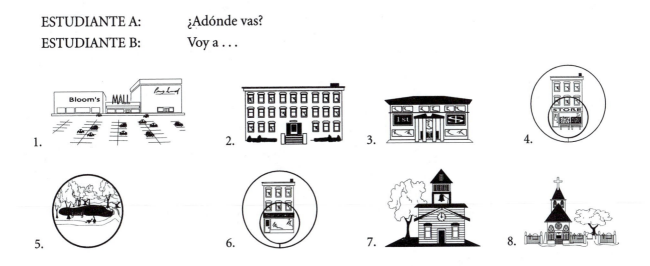

1.   2.   3.   4.

5.   6.   7.   8.

PART II RESIDENTIAL SITE TERMS

house
la casa

pool
la alberca

garage
el garaje

sidewalk
la banqueta

driveway
la calzada

front yard
el jardín de enfrente

back yard
el jardín de atrás

pond
el estanque

fountain
la fuente

street
la calle

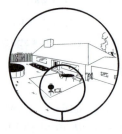

patio
el patio

dog
el perro

fence
la cerca

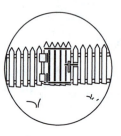

gate
la puerta

path
el sendero

MATCHING EXERCISE

Write the letter of the picture next to the Spanish word it matches.

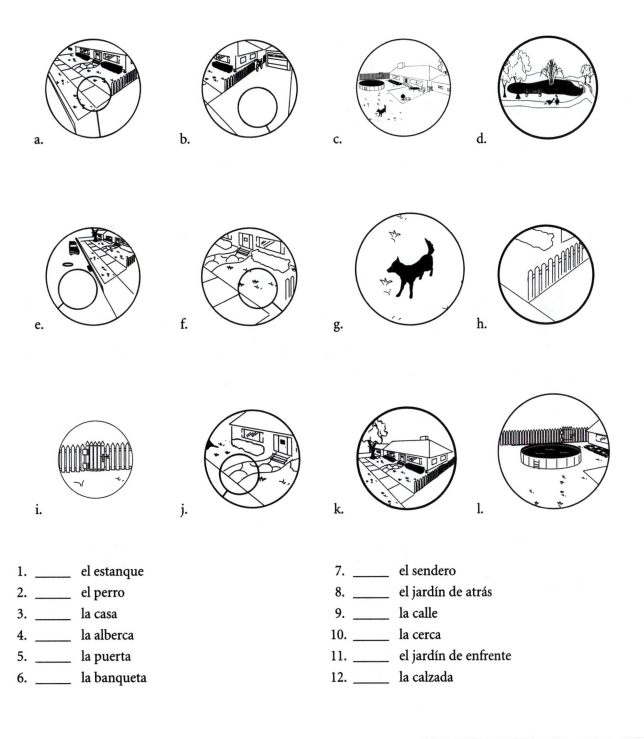

1. _____ el estanque
2. _____ el perro
3. _____ la casa
4. _____ la alberca
5. _____ la puerta
6. _____ la banqueta
7. _____ el sendero
8. _____ el jardín de atrás
9. _____ la calle
10. _____ la cerca
11. _____ el jardín de enfrente
12. _____ la calzada

VOCABULARY EXERCISE

Write the Spanish word for each picture in the space provided.

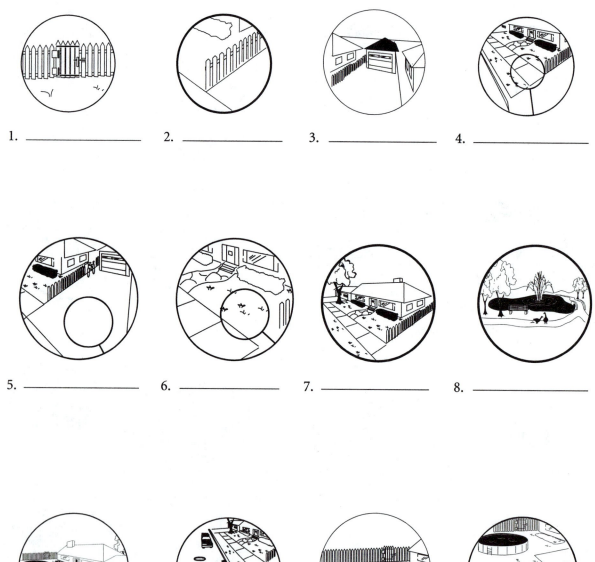

1. _____

2. _____

3. _____

4. _____

5. _____

6. _____

7. _____

8. _____

9. _____

10. _____

11. _____

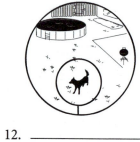

12. _____

MATCHING EXERCISE

Write the letter of the Spanish word next to the English word it matches on the left.

1. _____ sidewalk
2. _____ driveway
3. _____ front yard
4. _____ house
5. _____ pool
6. _____ garage
7. _____ back yard
8. _____ pond

9. _____ patio
10. _____ dog
11. _____ fence
12. _____ gate
13. _____ path
14. _____ fountain
15. _____ street

a. el jardín de atrás
b. el estanque
c. la fuente
d. el garaje
e. la cerca
f. la casa
g. la puerta
h. la banqueta

i. el sendero
j. el jardín de enfrente
k. la alberca
l. la calzada
m. la calle
n. el patio
o. el perro

CROSSWORD PUZZLES

Across

6. front yard
8. driveway
9. path
12. pool
13. dog
14. gate

Down

1. fountain
2. street
3. patio
4. house
5. sidewalk
6. back yard
7. pond
10. fence
11. garage

Across

3. perro
4. fuente
6. garaje
8. jardín de atrás
9. estanque
11. sendero
12. banqueta
13. cerca

Down

1. casa
2. patio
3. calzada
5. puerta
7. jardín de enfrente
10. alberca
12. calle

TRANSLATION EXERCISE

Translate the following to English:

1. la yarda atrás _____
2. el estanque _____
3. la fuente _____
4. el perro _____
5. la calzada _____
6. el jardín de enfrente _____
7. la calle _____
8. la cerca _____
9. la puerta _____
10. el patio _____
11. el sendero _____
12. la casa _____
13. la alberca _____
14. el garaje _____
15. la banqueta _____

Translate the following to Spanish:

1. pool _____
2. garage _____
3. sidewalk _____
4. driveway _____
5. house _____
6. back yard _____
7. gate _____
8. path _____
9. pond _____
10. patio _____
11. fountain _____
12. street _____
13. front yard _____
14. dog _____
15. fence _____

MULTIPLE CHOICE

Circle the letter of the correct answer.

1. **driveway**
   a. la calzada
   b. la calle
   c. la cerca
   d. la casa

2. **dog**
   a. la puerta
   b. el perro
   c. el patio
   d. la cerca

3. **house**
   a. la calzada
   b. la calle
   c. la cerca
   d. la casa

4. **back yard**
   a. la frente
   b. el jardín de enfrente
   c. el jardín de atrás
   d. la banqueta

5. **gate**
   a. la puerta
   b. la cerca
   c. la alberca
   d. la fuente

6. **path**
   a. la banqueta
   b. el sendero
   c. la estanque
   d. la calzada

7. **pond**
   a. el garaje
   b. la alberca
   c. la cerca
   d. el estanque

8. **pool**
   a. la puerta
   b. la cerca
   c. la alberca
   d. la fuente

9. **fence**
   a. la puerta
   b. la cerca
   c. la alberca
   d. la fuente

10. **sidewalk**
    a. la banqueta
    b. el sendero
    c. la alberca
    d. la calzada

11. **street**
    a. la calzada
    b. la calle
    c. la cerca
    d. la casa

12. **front yard**
    a. el jardín de enfrente
    b. la fuente
    c. el sendero
    d. el jardín de atrás

GRAMMAR: "GO" IN THE PAST TENSE

You recently learned to express where a person is going by using *voy, vas, vamos*. To speak about where someone went, you use the past tense. Study the examples.

Where did you go?	**¿Adónde fuiste?**
I went	**Fuí**
Joe went	**Fue**
We went	**Fuimos**

Translate the following to English:

1. Fuí _____

2. Fuimos _____

3. ¿Adónde fuiste? _____

4. Fue _____

5. Fuí _____

6. Fuimos _____

Translate the following to Spanish:

1. Where did you go? _____

2. I went _____

3. Mary went _____

4. We went _____

5. I went _____

6. Where did you go? _____

ROLE PLAY

Where did you go? Imagine it is Friday afternoon. Work with a partner. Ask and answer where you went at the site. Use the question ¿Adónde fuiste? Follow the model.

ESTUDIANTE A:	¿Adónde fuiste?
ESTUDIANTE B:	Fuí a…

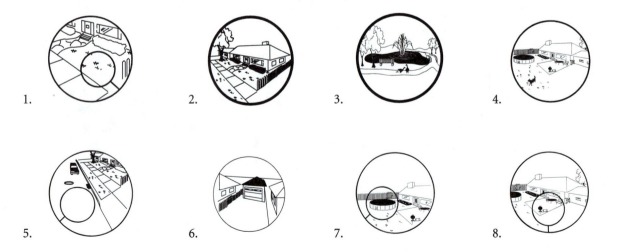

1.   2.   3.   4.

5.   6.   7.   8.

REVIEW

Translate the following to English:

1. ¿Adónde vas? _____
2. Voy a la yarda atrás. _____
3. Vamos a la iglesia. _____
4. Juan va a la tienda. _____
5. Voy a la escuela. _____
6. ¿Adónde fuiste? _____
7. Fui a la calzada. _____
8. Teresa fue al garaje. _____
9. Fuimos al edificio. _____
10. Ana fue a la alberca. _____

Translate the following to Spanish:

1. Where are you going? _____
2. I'm going to the store. _____
3. He's going to the bank. _____
4. We're going to the parking lot. _____
5. Where did you go? _____
6. I went to the parking lot. _____
7. We went to the back yard. _____
8. Thomas went to the bank. _____
9. We went to the house. _____
10. I went to the building. _____

Read the dialogue aloud with a partner and then translate it to English.

(viajando por camión)

Kevin: ¡Bienvenidos a Chicago!

Guillermo: Gracias, Kevin.

Kevin: ¿Te gusta escuchar música?

Guillermo: Sí, mucho. Me gusta la música salsa.

Kevin: Ayúdame.

Guillermo: (sintoniza al radio) ¿Qué hora es?

Kevin: Son las diez.

Guillermo: ¡Fántastico! (encuentra la estación del radio)

Kevin: Está bien. Me gusta la música.

Guillermo: ¿Adónde vas?

Kevin: Primero . . . a la iglesia católica.

Guillermo: ¿Hay misas (masses)?

Kevin: Sí . . . los domingos.

Guillermo: ¿A qué hora?

Kevin: A las ocho, diez, y doce.

Guillermo: ¿Vas a la iglesia, Kevin?

Kevin: Sí, voy con mi esposa y mis hijos.

Read the dialogue aloud with a partner and then translate it to Spanish.

(driving in the truck)

Kevin: Welcome to Chicago!

Guillermo: Thanks, Kevin.

Kevin: Do you like to listen to music?

Guillermo: Yes, a lot. I like salsa music.

Kevin: Help me.

Guillermo: (moves the dial) What time is it?

Kevin: It's ten o'clock.

Guillermo: Fantastic! (then finds the radio station)

Kevin: Okay. I like the music.

Guillermo: Where are you going?

Kevin: First . . . to the Catholic church.

Guillermo: Are there masses? (misas)

Kevin: Yes . . . on Sundays.

Guillermo: At what time?

Kevin: At eight, ten, and twelve o'clock.

Guillermo: Do you go to church, Kevin?

Kevin: Yes, I go with my wife and my children.

Guillermo: ¿Dónde está el banco?	**Guillermo:** Where is the bank?
Kevin: (señala) El edificio con ladrillo rojo.	**Kevin:** (points) The red brick building.
Guillermo: ¡Muy bien! Me gusta el estanque.	**Guillermo:** Very good! I like the pond.
Kevin: Gracias. ¿Te gustan las flores amarillas?	**Kevin:** Thank you. Do you like the yellow flowers?
Guillermo: ¡Sí, mucho! ¿Adónde vamos?	**Guillermo:** Yes, a lot! Where are we going?
Kevin: Vamos al hospital y los apartamentos.	**Kevin:** We're going to the hospital and the apartments.
(una hora más tarde en la casa de Kevin)	(an hour later at Kevin's house)
Kevin: ¿Dónde está tu mamá, Beth?	**Kevin:** Where is your mother, Beth?
Beth: Fue a la tienda.	**Beth:** She went to the store.
Kevin: Beth, quiero presentarte a Guillermo.	**Kevin:** Beth, I'd like to introduce you to Guillermo.
Beth: Nice to meet you.	**Beth:** Nice to meet you.
Kevin: No . . . recuerdas, Beth? . . . *"Mucho gusto"*	**Kevin:** No. . .remember, Beth? . . . *"Mucho gusto"*
Beth: Oh, yeah. ¡*Mucho gusto!*	**Beth:** Oh, yeah. ¡*Mucho gusto!*
Guillermo: ¡Igualmente!	**Guillermo:** Same to you!
Beth: ¿De dónde eres, Guillermo?	**Beth:** From where are you, Guillermo?

Translate the following to Spanish:

1. I'm studying Spanish. _____

2. Do you speak English? _____

3. Come with me. _____

4. You're a hard worker! _____

5. The crew is in a bad mood. _____

6. The manager is busy. _____

7. Get the blower. _____

8. Mix the oil and the gas. _____

9. Use the pick and the sledge hammer. _____

10. Be careful! Pay attention! Drive slowly! _____

11. Does your ankle hurt? Your back? _____

12. Miguel blows the leaves. _____

13. The crew prunes the shrubs. _____

14. My brother spreads out the mulch. _____

15. The crew leader applies the fertilizer. _____

CULTURE: NAMES AND NICKNAMES

The importance of the family in Latino culture is seen in the Spanish system of last names. The majority of Latinos have two last names. The system confuses many employees working in the personnel offices of United States organizations.

The father's name comes first followed by the mother's name. Juan Martinez López has a father whose surname is Martinez and a mother whose maiden name is López. If Juan's sister Ana marries Javier Hernández Rodriguez she keeps her father's name, drops her mother's name and becomes Ana Martinez Hernández.

Nicknames (apodos) are popular in both cultures. In English, the nickname for Robert is Bob, for William it's Bill and for Michael, Mike. In Spanish, common nicknames are Pepe for José, Paco for Francisco, and Memo for Guillermo. In English, young children often use the diminutive form of their name for example, *Pepito* to indicate "Young Pepe." In English, the name ends in -y or –ie and in Spanish the names end in –ito or –ita.

Many terms of endearment in the Latin culture may surprise Anglos. Gordo (chubby), flaco (skinny), and pelón (bald) are used often and affectionately with no intent to offend the person. In the United States it is the reverse. These type of nicknames are often used to be cruel.

A person's name is important to a person. It is important to learn to pronounce and spell your co-workers' names correctly.

Directions and Locations

PART I   DIRECTIONS

north	**norte**
south	**sur**
east	**este**
west	**oeste**
right	**derecha**
left	**izquierda**
straight ahead	**derecho**
only	**solamente**
here	**aquí**
around here	**por aquí**
there	**allí**
over there	**allá**
far	**lejos**
near	**cerca**

MATCHING EXERCISE

Write the letter of the Spanish word next to the English word it matches on the left.

1. _____ south
2. _____ there
3. _____ near
4. _____ right
5. _____ here
6. _____ west
7. _____ only

8. _____ east
9. _____ around here
10. _____ left
11. _____ over there
12. _____ far
13. _____ straight ahead
14. _____ north

a. derecha
b. lejos
c. aquí
d. sur
e. cerca
f. derecho
g. allá

h. oeste
i. allí
j. norte
k. solamente
l. este
m. izquierda
n. por aquí

CROSSWORD PUZZLES

Across

1. far
4. right
5. around here
7. south
8. only
11. left
12. near

Down

2. west
3. over there
4. straight ahead
6. east
9. here
10. north
13. there

TEAM BUILDING TIP

During the holidays, give your Latino workers a phone card to call their families. The directions on how to use them are printed in English as well as in Spanish.

Across

1. cerca
3. allá
5. aquí
8. sur
10. oeste
11. derecho
13. solamente

Down

1. norte
2. derecha
4. allí
6. este
7. izquierda
9. lejos
12. por aquí

TRANSLATION EXERCISE

Translate the following to English:

1. norte _____

2. sur _____

3. lejos _____

4. cerca _____

5. derecha _____

6. izquierda _____

7. derecho _____

8. este _____

9. oeste _____

10. aquí _____

11. allí _____

12. por aquí _____

13. allá _____

14. solamente _____

Translate the following to Spanish:

1. near _____

2. far _____

3. north _____

4. south _____

5. here _____

6. around here _____

7. there _____

8. over there _____

9. straight ahead _____

10. left _____

11. right _____

12. east _____

13. west _____

14. only _____

MULTIPLE CHOICE

Circle the letter of the correct answer.

1. **near**
   a. norte
   b. sur
   c. lejos
   d. cerca

2. **right**
   a. derecha
   b. izquierda
   c. derecho
   d. este

3. **here**
   a. allá
   b. aquí
   c. allí
   d. por aquí

4. **only**
   a. solamente
   b. oeste

   c. derecho
   d. este

5. **far**
   a. norte
   b. sur
   c. lejos
   d. cerca

6. **left**
   a. derecha
   b. izquierda
   c. derecho
   d. lejos

7. **over there**
   a. aquí
   b. allí
   c. por aquí
   d. allá

8. **here**
   a. este
   b. oeste
   c. aquí
   d. allí

9. **west**
   a. este
   b. oeste
   c. aquí
   d. allí

10. **only**
    a. oeste
    b. aquí
    c. solamente
    d. allá

PART II   LOCATIONS

in, on
en

on top
encima

up, above
arriba

down, below
abajo

in front
delante

behind
detrás

between
entre

around
alrededor

inside
dentro

outside
fuera

over
sobre

MATCHING EXERCISE

Write the letter of each picture next to the Spanish word it matches below.

 a.

 b.

 c.

 d.

 e.

 f.

 g.

 h.

 i.

1. _____ encima
2. _____ arriba
3. _____ delante
4. _____ alrededor
5. _____ abajo

6. _____ dentro
7. _____ entre
8. _____ detrás
9. _____ fuera

VOCABULARY EXERCISE

Write the Spanish word for each picture in the space provided.

1. _____

2. _____

3. _____

4. _____

5. _____

6. _____

7. _____

8. _____

9. _____

MATCHING EXERCISE

Write the letter of the Spanish word next to the English word it matches on the left.

1. _____ between
2. _____ over
3. _____ on top
4. _____ up, above
5. _____ in front

6. _____ outside
7. _____ down, below
8. _____ around
9. _____ inside
10. _____ behind

a. abajo
b. alrededor
c. dentro
d. detrás
e. entre

f. sobre
g. encima
h. arriba
i. delante
j. fuera

CROSSWORD PUZZLES

Across

2. down, below
5. in, on
6. behind
8. around
10. on top

Down

1. outside
2. up, above
3. inside
4. between
7. over
9. in front

Across

2. sobre
5. entre
6. encima
7. dentro

Down

1. detrás
2. fuera
3. delante
4. alrededor

TRANSLATION EXERCISE

Translate the following to English:

1. dentro _____
2. arriba _____
3. sobre _____
4. fuera _____
5. alrededor _____
6. detrás _____
7. delante _____
8. entre _____
9. abajo _____
10. encima _____

Translate the following to Spanish:

1. between _____
2. over _____
3. on top _____
4. up, above _____
5. in front _____
6. outside _____
7. down, below _____
8. around _____
9. inside _____
10. behind _____

MULTIPLE CHOICE

Circle the letter of the correct answer.

1. outside
- a. dentro
- b. arriba
- c. sobre
- d. fuera

2. in front
- a. alrededor
- b. detrás
- c. delante
- d. entre

3. down, below
- a. abajo
- b. encima
- c. detrás
- d. delante

4. up, above
- a. dentro
- b. alrededor
- c. sobre
- d. arriba

5. behind
- a. detrás
- b. delante
- c. fuera
- d. entre

6. around
- a. abajo
- b. en
- c. alrededor
- d. encima

7. in, on
- a. encima
- b. en
- c. entre
- d. abajo

8. between
- a. entre
- b. en
- c. encima
- d. sobre

9. outside
- a. dentro
- b. delante
- c. fuera
- d. arriba

10. over
- a. arriba
- b. sobre
- c. delante
- d. detrás

ROLE PLAY

Beware of Dog! Many residential sites have dogs. Pretend that you are afraid of them. Working with a partner, ask and answer where the dog is located. Follow the model.

| ESTUDIANTE A: | ¿Dónde está el perro? |
| ESTUDIANTE B: | El perro está en la casa. |

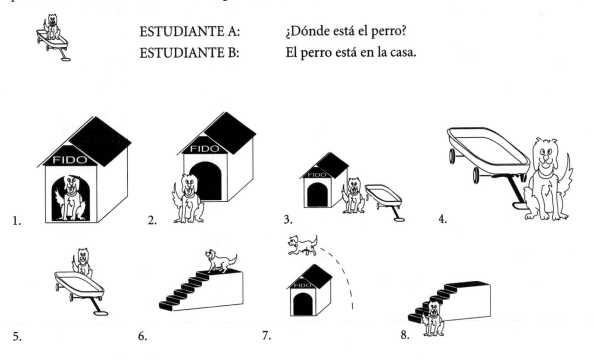

REVIEW

Translate the following to Spanish:

1. Where is the house? _____

2. The house is not far, it's close. _____

3. The house is over there. _____

4. Where? Straight ahead? _____

5. On the left? No, on the right. _____

6. Where is the dog? _____

7. The dog is inside the house. _____

8. No, the dog is behind the house. _____

9. The dog is outside! _____

10. Yes, the dog is here! _____

Read the dialogue aloud with a partner and then translate it to English.

(alrededor de la cafetera)

Randy: Hola. Buenos días, Juanito.

Juanito: Hola, jefe. ¿Cómo estás?

Randy: ¡Excelente! ¡Estoy de buen humor!

Juanito: ¿Por qué?

Randy: ¡Porque hoy es mi cumpleaños!

Juanito: ¿El 29 de febrero? Hay solamente 28 días en febrero. . .

Randy: No. ¡Es Leap Year! ¡Tengo solamente siete años!

(en el parque de aparcamiento)

Randy: Por favor, vete a Tall Trees Nursery.

Juanito: ¿Qué quieres?

Randy: Necesito un saco de tierra, turba, mezcla y fertilizante.

Juanito: ¿Necesitas piedras, ladrillos y cemento?

Randy: Sí.

Juanito: Es mucho. Ven conmigo. ¡Por favor!

Randy: No. . .no. . .estoy muy ocupado.

Read the dialogue aloud with a partner and then translate it to Spanish.

(at the coffee pot)

Randy: Hello. Good morning, Juanito.

Juanito: Hello, boss. How are you?

Randy: Excellent! I'm in a good mood!

Juanito: Why?

Randy: Because it's my birthday!

Juanito: The 29th of February? There are only 28 days in February. . .

Randy: No. It's Leap Year! I'm only seven years old!

(in the parking lot)

Randy: Please, go to Tall Trees Nursery.

Juanito: What do you want?

Randy: I need a bag of soil, peat moss, mulch, and fertilizer.

Juanito: Do you need stones, bricks, and cement?

Randy: Yes.

Juanito: It's a lot! Come with me. Please!

Randy: No. . .no. . .I'm very busy.

Juanito: ¿Adónde vas?	**Juanito:** Where are you going?
Randy: Voy a la oficina.	**Randy:** I'm going to the office.
(una hora más tarde)	(an hour later)
Randy: Gracias, Juanito. Eres muy trabajador!	**Randy:** Thanks, Juanito. You're a hard worker!
Juanito: ¡Y muy responsable!	**Juanito:** And very responsible!
Randy: Sí. . .por eso eres el mayordomo.	**Randy:** Yes. . .it's why you're the foreman.
Juanito: Soy mayordomo porque hablo inglés, ¿no?	**Juanito:** I'm the foreman because I speak English, right?
Randy: Sí. Juanito estudio español.	**Randy:** Yes. Juanito. . . I study Spanish.
Juanito: ¿Como se dice "You're smart for a seven-year-old?" en español?	**Juanito:** How do you say "You're smart for a seven-year-old?" in Spanish?
Randy: ¡Eres inteligente para tener 7 años! ¿Cómo se dice "Let's go!" en español?	**Randy:** Eres muy inteligente por siete años! How do you say "Let's go!" in Spanish?
Juanito: ¡Vamos!	**Juanito:** ¡Vamos!
Randy: Vamos al mall, primero.	**Randy:** Let's go to the mall, first.
Juanito: ¿Dónde está?	**Juanito:** Where is it?
Randy: Está por aquí.	**Randy:** It's around here.
Juanito: Oh. . . sí. . . cerca de McDonald's.	**Juanito:** Oh. . . yes. . . near the McDonald's.
Randy: ¿Quieres comer?	**Randy:** Do you want to eat?
Juanito: Sí. . .	**Juanito:** Yes. . .
Drive thru: Hola! ¡Buenas tardes! ¿Qué quieres?	**Drive thru:** Hello! Good afternoon! What would you like?
Randy: Quiero cuatro hamburguesas y dos Cocas.	**Randy:** I want four hamburgers and two Cokes.
Drive thru: Séis dólares, por favor.	**Drive thru:** Six dollars, please.
Randy: Gracias.	**Randy:** Thank you.
Juanito: Randy, aquí es tres dólares.	**Juanito:** Randy, here is three dollars.
Randy: No. . .no. . . comprame una cerveza para mi cumpleaños!	**Randy:** No. . . no. . . buy me a beer for my birthday!
Juanito: ¿Hay una fiesta?	**Juanito:** Is there a party?
Randy: Sí. . . en mi casa. ¡Alrededor de la alberca! Y en la alberca. ¡Vamos a jugar volibol en el agua!	**Randy:** Yes. . . at my house. Around the pool! And in the pool. We're going to play volleyball in the water!
Randy: ¿Te gusta nadar?	**Randy:** Do you like to swim?
Juanito: ¡Me gusta mucho! ¿Dónde está tu casa?	**Juanito:** I like to a lot! Where is your house?
Randy: Mi casa está entre las calles Oak y Maple.	**Randy:** My house is between Oak and Maple Streets.
Juanito: ¿Detrás de la iglesia y el aparcamiento?	**Juanito:** Behind the church and the parking lot?

Randy: Sí. La fiesta es el viernes a las ocho.
(viernes)

Randy: Por favor. . .poda los arbustos, sopla las hojas, y riega las flores.

Juanito: ¿Y barre la banqueta? ¿Con la escoba o el cepillo?

Randy: No me importa. ¡Estoy nervioso!

Juanito: ¿Adónde vas?

Randy: Voy a la tienda. Necesito pizza, ensalada, Coca y cerveza.

Juanito: ¡Y hielo!
*hielo – ice

Randy: Yes. The party is on Friday at 8:00.
(Friday)

Randy: Please . . . prune the shrubs, blow the leaves, and water the flowers.

Juanito: And sweep the sidewalk? With the broom or the push broom?

Randy: I don't care. I'm nervous!

Juanito: Where are you going?

Randy: I'm going to the store. I need pizza, salad, Coke, and beer.

Juanito: And ice *!
*ice – el hielo

Translate the following to Spanish:

1. How's it going? _____

2. Do you speak English? _____

3. Everything else is perfect! _____

4. When? Who? With whom? How many? _____

5. First go to the store and the bank. _____

6. Second go to the parking lots. _____

7. Monday, Friday, Saturday, Sunday _____

8. What's your wife's name? _____

9. The woman is patient. The man is impatient. _____

10. I play billiards on Fridays. Do you like to play? _____

11. My shoulder hurts. Does your neck hurt? _____

12. Drive slowly. Don't touch the blades. _____

13. Wash and put away the shovels and the pruners. _____

14. Plant, water, and mulch the trees. _____

15. Blow and rake the leaves. _____

16. Spread and tamp the soil. Add the mulch. _____

17. Get the stones and the rock. _____

18. Tag the names. Tag the prices. _____

19. Repot the yellow annuals in plastic pots. _____

20. Deadhead the plants. _____

CULTURE: INDEPENDENCE DAYS

Country	Independence Day	Country	Independence Day
United States	July 4	Guatemala	September 15
Argentina	July 9	Honduras	September 15
Bolivia	August 6	Mexico	September 16
Chile	September 18	Nicaragua	September 15
Colombia	July 20	Panama	November 28 (from Spain)
Costa Rica	September 15		November 3 (from Colombia)
Cuba	May 20	Paraguay	May 14
Dominican Republic	February 22	Peru	July 28
Ecuador	October 3	Uruguay	August 25
El Salvador	September 15	Venezuela	July 5

HOLIDAYS

January 6: Feast of the Epiphany is the day the Three Kings bring gifts to Latino children.

March–April: Semana Santa (Holy Week), the week leading to Easter Sunday, is observed with parades and passion plays.

May 1: Labor Day is a day for workers to parade through the streets.

May 5: Cinco de Mayo marks, with great fanfare countrywide, the anniversary of the French defeat by Mexican troops in Puebla in 1862.

June 24: Saint John the Baptist Day, a popular national holiday, sees many Mexicans observing a tradition of tossing a "blessing" of water on most anyone within reach!

August 15: Feast of the Assumption of the Blessed Virgin Mary is celebrated nationwide with religious processions.

November 1–2: On el Día de los Muertos, families welcome back the spirits of departed relatives to elaborate altars and refurbished gravesites.

December 12: On Feast Day of the Virgin of Guadalupe, Mexico's patron saint is honored with processions and native folk dances.

13

Watering, Spraying, and Irrigation

PART I TERMS TO USE WITH WATERING, SPRAYING, AND IRRIGATION

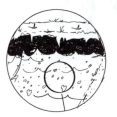
water
el agua

soil
la tierra

hose
la manguera

trench
la zanja

pipe
la pipa

elbow
el codo

leak
la fuga

nozzle
la boquilla

valve
la válvula

sprinkler heads
las cabezas

wire
el alambre

sprinkler
el rociador

MATCHING EXERCISE

Write the letter of each picture next to the Spanish word it matches below.

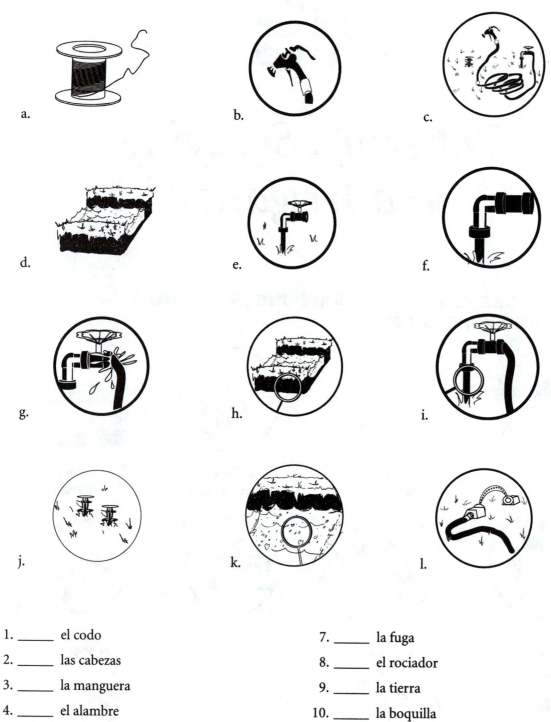

a.

b.

c.

d.

e.

f.

g.

h.

i.

j.

k.

l.

1. _____ el codo

2. _____ las cabezas

3. _____ la manguera

4. _____ el alambre

5. _____ el agua

6. _____ la zanja

7. _____ la fuga

8. _____ el rociador

9. _____ la tierra

10. _____ la boquilla

11. _____ la pipa

12. _____ la válvula

VOCABULARY EXERCISE

Write the Spanish word for each picture in the space provided.

1. _____

2. _____

3. _____

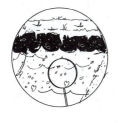

4. _____

5. _____

6. _____

7. _____

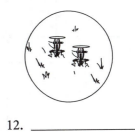

8. _____

9. _____

10. _____

11. _____

12. _____

CROSSWORD PUZZLES

Across

3. water
7. hose
8. soil
10. pipe
11. elbow
12. sprinkler heads

Down

1. wire
2. valve
4. leak
5. nozzle
6. trench
9. sprinkler

Across

2. agua
6. pipa
7. rociador
8. boquilla
9. manguera
12. fuga

Down

1. tierra
3. zanja
4. cable, alambre
5. cabezas
10. codo
11. válvula

Translate the following to English:

1. la fuga _____
2. las cabezas _____
3. la zanja _____
4. el alambre _____
5. la válvula _____
6. la fuga _____
7. la pipa _____
8. el rociador _____
9. la boquilla _____
10. la manguera _____

Translate the following to Spanish:

1. leak _____
2. sprinkler _____
3. wire _____
4. pipe _____
5. water _____
6. nozzle _____
7. valve _____
8. trench _____
9. elbow _____
10. sprinkler heads _____

MULTIPLE CHOICE

Circle the letter of the correct answer.

1. **leak**
   a. la zanja
   b. la tierra
   c. el codo
   d. la fuga, el escape

2. **soil**
   a. la boquilla
   b. la manguera
   c. la tierra
   d. la zanja

3. **water**
   a. la pipa
   b. el rociador
   c. el agua
   d. la manguera

4. **hose**
   a. la manguera
   b. el rociador
   c. el agua
   d. la boquilla

5. **trench**
   a. la baquilla
   b. la manguera
   c. la tierra
   d. la zanja

6. **elbow**
   a. la pipa
   b. el codo
   c. la fuga
   d. la tierra

7. **pipe**
   a. el alambre
   b. la válvula
   c. la zanja
   d. la pipa

8. **nozzle**
   a. la baquilla
   b. la manguera
   c. la tierra
   d. la zanja

9. **valve**
   a. la zanja
   b. la tierra
   c. el codo
   d. la válvula

10. **wire**
    a. el alambre
    b. la válvula
    c. la zanja
    d. la manguera

11. **sprinkler heads**
    a. el agua
    b. el rociador
    c. las cabezas
    d. el alambre

12. **sprinkler**
    a. el agua
    b. el rociador
    c. las cabezas
    d. el alambre

PART II ACTIONS TO USE WITH WATERING, SPRAYING, AND IRRIGATION

Group 1		Group 2	
dig	**excava**	get	**consigue**
cut	**corta**	adjust	**ajusta**
hold	**agarra**	connect	**conecta**
install	**instala**	push	**empuja**
open	**abre**	pack	**empaca**
smooth out	**empareja**	close	**cierra**

Other Irrigation Words

check	**checa**
flush	**saca el agua**
pull	**jala**
put	**pon**
replace	**reemplaza**

TEAM BUILDING TIP

Upon their arrival to your company, give the Latinos a Catholic church bulletin so they know where and when the masses are. Advertise in it, too, so you can find other Latino employees.

Assign each of your Anglo employees to help one or two Latino workers. Involve everyone in the company, not just the people working on site with them.

GROUP 1

Matching Exercise

Write the letter of the Spanish word next to the English word it matches on the left.

1. _____ install   a. abre
2. _____ dig   b. agarra
3. _____ hold   c. corta
4. _____ smooth out d. instala
5. _____ open   e. excava
6. _____ cut   f. empareja

Translate the following to English:

1. instala _____
2. abre _____
3. corta _____
4. agarra _____
5. empareja _____
6. excava _____

Translate the following to Spanish:

1. open _____
2. smooth out _____
3. dig _____
4. install _____
5. hold _____
6. cut _____

GROUP 2

Matching Exercise

Write the letter of the Spanish word next to the English word it matches on the left.

1. _____ adjust   a. empuja
2. _____ close   b. consigue
3. _____ push   c. empaca
4. _____ get   d. conecta
5. _____ pack   e. cierra
6. _____ connect   f. ajusta

Translate the following to English:

1. consigue _____
2. ajusta _____
3. empaca _____
4. cierra _____
5. conecta _____
6. empuja _____

Translate the following to Spanish:

1. pack _____
2. connect _____
3. close _____
4. adjust _____
5. get _____
6. push _____

CROSSWORD PUZZLES

Across

2. cut
4. connect
8. dig
10. push
11. hold
12. smooth out
14. pack

Down

1. get
3. replace
5. close
6. adjust
7. install
9. open
13. pull

Across

1. empaca
3. corta
5. excava
7. abre
8. reemplaza
9. empuja
10. instala
12. agarra

Down

2. cierra
3. conecta
4. ajusta
6. consigue
9. jala
11. empareja

MULTIPLE CHOICE

Circle the letter of the correct answer.

1. **dig**
   a. corta
   b. consigue
   c. excava
   d. empaca

2. **install**
   a. ajusta
   b. instala
   c. cierra
   d. abre

3. **hold**
   a. agarra
   b. ajusta
   c. instala
   d. cierra

4. **open**
   a. ajusta
   b. instala
   c. cierra
   d. abre

5. **cut**
   a. conecta
   b. corta
   c. cierra
   d. consigue

6. **smooth out**
   a. empareja
   b. empaca
   c. empuja
   d. agarra

7. **adjust**
   a. instala
   b. corta
   c. excava
   d. ajusta

8. **get**
   a. conecta
   b. corta
   c. cierra
   d. consigue

9. **push**
   a. empareja
   b. empaca
   c. empuja
   d. agarra

10. **connect**
    a. conecta
    b. corta
    c. cierra
    d. consigue

11. **close**
    a. empaca
    b. abre
    c. agarra
    d. cierra

12. **pack**
    a. excava
    b. empareja
    c. empuja
    d. empaca

GRAMMAR: CAN YOU? ARE YOU ABLE?

To ask if someone is able to do something, use the word *Puedes* plus the -ar ending of the action word to make the request.

Study the examples.

Can you? Are you able?	¿Puedes?
Yes, I can.	Sí, puedo.
No, I cannot.	No, no puedo.
Can you work on Saturday?	¿Puedes **trabajar** el sábado?
Can you adjust the valve?	¿Puedes **ajustar** la válvula?
Can you connect the pipe?	¿Puedes **conectar** la pipa?

ROLE PLAY

Our Busy Season! Pretend it's Spring and everyone wants everything now! Ask your co-worker if he can work extra days this month. Use the phrase ¿Puedes? Follow the model.

ESTUDIANTE A: ¿Puedes trabajar el martes?
ESTUDIANTE B: Sí, puedo.
                  No, no puedo.

Sunday domingo	Monday lunes	Tuesday martes	Wednesday miércoles	Thursday jueves	Friday viernes	Saturday sábado
	1	2	3	4	5	6
7	8	9	10	11	12	13
14	15	16	17	18	19	20
21	22	23	24	25	26	27
28	29	30	31			

Sunday	**domingo**
Monday	**lunes**
Tuesday	**martes**
Wednesday	**miércoles**
Thursday	**jueves**
Friday	**viernes**
Saturday	**sábado**

REVIEW

Translate the following to English:

1. Corta la pipa. _____

2. Excava la zanja. _____

3. Abre el agua. _____

4. Empaca la tierra. _____

5. Pon las boquillas. _____

6. Ajusta las cabezas. _____

7. Empareja la tierra. _____

8. Empuja la pipa. _____

9. ¿Puedes conectar la pipa?. _____

10. ¿Puedes instalar las cabezas?. _____

Translate the following to Spanish:

1. Check the soil. _____

2. Dig a trench. _____

3. Close the valve. _____

4. Install the pipe. _____

5. Adjust the valves. _____

6. Push the pipe. _____

7. Connect the heads. _____

8. Pack the soil. _____

9. Adjust the heads. Can you adjust the heads? _____

10. Cut the pipe. Can you cut the pipe? _____

Read the dialogue aloud with a partner and then translate it to English.

(lunes, el 7 de julio)

Chris: ¿Puedes trabajar el sábado, Juan?

Juan: ¿Por qué? ¿Estás muy ocupado?

Chris: Sí.

Juan: ¿A qué hora?

Chris: A las seis y media... ¿Es posible?

Juan: Sí. A las seis y media el 12 de julio.

Chris: Es correcto. ¿Puedes trabajar el domingo?

Juan: No, Chris. Los domingos voy a la iglesia con mi esposa y mis hijos.

(sábado, el 12 de julio)

Chris: Ten cuidado y presta atención.

Juan: ¿Hay muchos cables y alambre?

Chris: Sí. Muchos...red, blue, green, yellow...

Juan: ¿Cómo se dice los colores en español?

Read the dialogue aloud with a partner and then translate it to Spanish.

(Monday, July 7)

Chris: Can you work on Saturday, Juan?

Juan: Why? Are you busy?

Chris: Yes.

Juan: At what time?

Chris: At six thirty... Is that possible?

Juan: Sí. At six thirty on July 12th.

Chris: That's correct. Can you work on Sunday?

Juan: No, Chris. On Sundays I go to church with my wife and my children.

(Saturday, July 12)

Chris: Be careful and pay attention.

Juan: Are there many cables and wires?

Chris: Yes. Many... red, blue, green, yellow ...

Juan: How do you say the colors in Spanish?

Chris: Hmmm. . .estudio español. . . rojo, azul, verde, negro, gris, blanco, café, amarillo, rosado, morado y. . . ana. . . anaran. . .

Juan: ¡Hazlo como yo! A- na -ran- ja- do.

Chris: A-na-ran-ja-do. Anaranjado.

Juan: Correcto. ¡Perfecto!

Chris: ¿Excavaste una zanja?

Juan: Sí. Y la cuadrilla está cansada.

Chris: Vamos a comer y beber mucho agua.

Juan: Amigos. . .¡Atención ! Vamos a comer.
(a las dos y media)

Chris: Okay. Primero, jala la pipa.

Juan: Segundo, ¿Conecta las cabezas?

Chris: Es correcto. Instala las válvulas.

Juan: ¿Ajusta las válvulas?

Chris: Sí. Y empaca la tierra.

Juan: Está bien. Soy muy responsable.

Chris: Sí. Eres muy trabajador. Gracias.
(Al final del día)

Chris: ¿Conectaste la pipa?

Juan: Sí.

Chris: ¿Instalaste las cabezas?

Juan: Sí.

Chris: ¿Ajustaste las válvulas?

Juan: Sí.

Chris: Estás nervioso, Juan. ¿Hay problemas?

Juan: Ah . . . hay . . . hay una fuga.

Chris: ¿Una fuga? ¿Dónde? ¿Puedes trabaja el domingo?

Chris: Hmmm. . .I'm studying Spanish. . . rojo, azul, verde, negro, gris, blanco, café, amarillo, rosado, morado y. . . ana. . . anaran. . .

Juan: Do it like me! A- na -ran- ja- do.

Chris: A-na-ran-ja-do. Anaranjado.

Juan: Correct. Perfect!

Chris: Did you dig a ditch?

Juan: Yes. And the crew is tired.

Chris: Let's go eat and drink a lot of water.

Juan: Amigos. . .Attention! We're going to eat.
(at two thirty)

Chris: Okay. First, pull the pipe.

Juan: Second, connect the heads?

Chris: That's correct. And install the valves.

Juan: Adjust the valves?

Chris: Yes. And pack the soil.

Juan: Okay. I'm very responsible.

Chris: Yes. You are very hardworking. Thank you.
(at the end of the day)

Chris: Did you connect the pipe?

Juan: Yes.

Chris: Did you install the heads?

Juan: Yes.

Chris: Did you adjust the valves?

Juan: Yes.

Chris: You're nervous, Juan. Are there problems?

Juan: Ah. . .there is. . .there is a leak.

Chris: A leak? Where? Can you work on Sunday?

Translate the following to Spanish:

1. How's the family? _____

2. I'm studying Spanish. _____

3. Try it. Keep trying. _____

4. How many pizzas are there? There are four. _____

5. Fantastic! Incredible! Fabulous! _____

6. There are twenty four hours in a day. _____

7. The crew is sensitive. The crew is in a bad mood. _____

8. The woman is the boss. The man is a technician. _____

9. My uncle is responsible. My aunt is hardworking. _____

10. Do you like to play soccer? Where? When? _____

11. My head hurts. Does your ankle hurt? _____

12. Wear your uniform. Wash your uniform. _____

13. Wash and put away the wheelbarrow. _____

14. First, deadhead the white flowers. _____

15. Second, fertilize and water the plants. _____

16. Spread and tamp the soil. Add the mulch. _____

17. Get the red bricks and the gray stones. _____

18. Tag the names. Tag the prices. _____

19. Repot the purple perennials in clay pots. _____

20. Where? Left? Right? Between? Behind? _____

Other Useful Irrigation Terms

pipe sizes	tamaños de pipa, tubo	forty-five	cuarenta y cinco grados
half inch	media pulgada		
three quarters	tres cuartos	coupling	la junta, la conexión
one inch	una pulgada	cap	el casquillo de pipa, tubo
one and a quarter	una y cuarto		
one and a half	una y media	ditch	la zanja
two inches	dos pulgadas	deep	profundo, hondo
three inches	tres pulgadas	deeper	más profundo, más hondo
pipe fittings	las conexiones		
threaded pipe	la pipa roscada	shallow	poco profundo, bajo
nipple	el niple	wet	mojado
elbow	el codo	dry	seco
tee	la "T"	mud	el lodo
ninety degrees	el codo de noventa grados	above ground	sobre tierra
		below ground	bajo tierra

CULTURE: IMMIGRANT LABOR

During times of low unemployment, labor is difficult to find. Many organizations hire foreign-born employees. If an employer is unsure of the steps to take in hiring them, the U. S. Immigration and Naturalization Service (INS) will send out a handbook that explains hiring guidelines. The INS can be contacted at: www.usdoj.gov/ins/.

Penalties for "knowingly" hiring illegal workers and being audited by the INS can be stiff, so many organizations are hiring employees from Mexico through the United States government's H-2B program. The program is specifically intended for seasonal, temporary employment. Getting employees from Mexico is a bit time consuming and expensive, yet it is worth the effort in the long run.

The process takes approximately 120 days and involves two major steps: (1) finding and recruiting the workers, and (2) completing the paperwork to allow them to come to the United States and work for your organization for seasonal or temporary work.

A person can follow the process alone, but using professional help is suggested. There are many H-2B employment services that are available to help an organization recruit Latino workers and complete the necessary paperwork.

TEAM BUILDING TIP

Rent the video *El Norte* (The North) and experience what many Latinos feel as they leave their homeland and head to the United States with high hopes. The story is about a brother and sister who leave Guatemala, travel north through Mexico, and finally arrive in Los Angeles. It is in English.

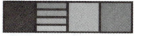

14

Golf Course and Fishing Terms and Actions

PART I   GOLF COURSE TERMS

golf course
el campo de golf

ball marks
las marcas de bola

divots
las raspadas

bunker
la trampa

geese
los gansos

geese poop
la mierda de los gansos

flags
las banderas

hole, cup
el hoyo, la copa

men's tee
el tee de hombres

women's tee
el tee de mujeres

players
los jugadores

members
los miembros

golf cart
el carrito

driving range
la área de práctica

garbage
la basura

MATCHING EXERCISE

Write the letter of each picture next to the Spanish word it matches below.

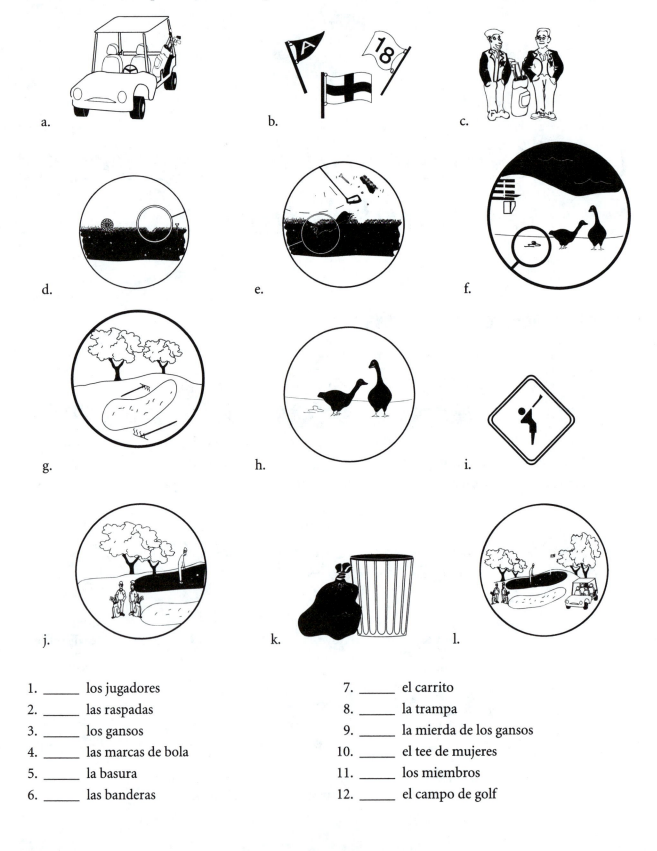

a.

b.

c.

d.

e.

f.

g.

h.

i.

j.

k.

l.

1. _____ los jugadores
2. _____ las raspadas
3. _____ los gansos
4. _____ las marcas de bola
5. _____ la basura
6. _____ las banderas

7. _____ el carrito
8. _____ la trampa
9. _____ la mierda de los gansos
10. _____ el tee de mujeres
11. _____ los miembros
12. _____ el campo de golf

VOCABULARY EXERCISE

Write the Spanish word for each picture in the space provided.

1. _____

2. _____

3. _____

4. _____

5. _____

6. _____

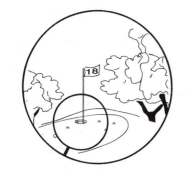

9. _____

7. _____

8. _____

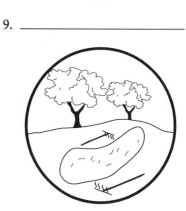

10. _____

11. _____

12. _____

MATCHING EXERCISE

Write the letter of the Spanish word next to the English word it matches on the left.

1. _____ divots	9. _____ golf cart	a. las marcas de bola	i. la trampa
2. _____ bunker	10. _____ driving range	b. el carrito	j. el hoyo, la copa
3. _____ men's tee	11. _____ geese poop	c. la mierda de los gansos	k. el tee de hombres
4. _____ golf course	12. _____ players	d. las banderas	l. la basura
5. _____ geese	13. _____ members	e. las raspadas	m. el tee de mujeres
6. _____ ball marks	14. _____ garbage	f. el campo de golf	n. los gansos
7. _____ women's tee	15. _____ flags	g. los miembros	o. los jugadores
8. _____ hole, cup		h. la área de práctica	

CROSSWORD PUZZLES

Across

2. women's tee
4. bunker
7. golf cart
9. members
11. geese
12. garbage
14. hole
15. driving range

Down

1. flags
3. players
5. divots
6. geese poop
8. men's tee
10. ball marks
13. golf course

Across

4. tee de mujeres
6. jugadores
8. área de práctica
10. gansos
11. banderas
12. marcas de bola
13. miembros

Down

1. hoyo
2. tee de hombres
3. carrito
5. raspadas
7. basura
9. mierda de los gansos
10. campo de golf
12. trampa

TRANSLATION EXERCISE

Translate the following to English:

1. las marcas de bola _____
2. las raspadas _____
3. la trampa _____
4. el tee de hombres _____
5. el campo de golf _____
6. la mierda de los gansos _____
7. los miembros _____
8. el carrito _____
9. el tee de mujeres _____
10. el hoyo, la copa _____
11. los jugadores _____
12. la basura _____
13. los gansos _____
14. la área de práctica _____
15. las banderas _____

Translate the following to Spanish:

1. golf course _____
2. geese poop _____
3. ball marks _____
4. divots _____
5. bunker _____
6. men's tee _____
7. women's tee _____
8. hole, cup _____
9. players _____
10. members _____
11. golf cart _____
12. driving range _____
13. flags _____
14. garbage _____
15. geese _____

MULTIPLE CHOICE

Circle the letter of the correct answer.

1. flags
   a. las banderas
   b. los gansos
   c. la basura
   d. las raspadas

2. golf cart
   a. la trampa
   b. la mierda de los gansos
   c. los miembros
   d. el carrito

3. players
   a. los jugadores
   b. los gansos
   c. la basura
   d. las raspadas

4. members
   a. los gansos
   b. los miembros
   c. los jugadores
   d. las raspadas

5. garbage
   a. los jugadores
   b. los gansos
   c. la basura
   d. las raspadas

6. ball marks
   a. las marcas de bola
   b. la trampa
   c. la basura
   d. las raspadas

7. divots
   a. los jugadores
   b. los gansos
   c. la basura
   d. las raspadas

8. bunker
   a. las marcas de bola
   b. las raspadas
   c. la basura
   d. la trampa

9. geese
   a. los jugadores
   b. los gansos
   c. la basura
   d. las raspadas

10. geese poop
   a. la mierda de los gansos
   b. las marcas de bola
   c. los gansos
   d. los miembros

ACTIONS TO USE WITH GOLF / TURFGRASS

repair	**repara**
pick up	**recoge**
scare	**asusta**
smile	**sonríe**
cut	**corta**
rake	**rastrilla**

MATCHING EXERCISE

Write the letter of the Spanish word next to the English word it matches on the left.

1. _____ repair   a. sonríe
2. _____ pick up   b. rastrilla
3. _____ scare   c. repara
4. _____ smile   d. asusta
5. _____ cut   e. recoge
6. _____ rake   f. corta

Translate the following to English:

1. recoge _____
2. corta _____
3. sonríe _____
4. rastrilla _____
5. repara _____
6. asusta _____

Translate the following to Spanish:

1. scare _____
2. smile _____
3. repair _____
4. pick up _____
5. cut _____
6. rake _____

Translate the following to English:

1. Recoge la basura. _____
2. Corta los hoyos. _____
3. Sonríe a los miembros. _____
4. Rastrilla las trampas. _____
5. Recoge las banderas. _____
6. Repara las raspadas. _____
7. Asusta los gansos. _____
8. Recoge la mierda de los gansos. _____
9. Sonríe a los jugadores. _____
10. Repara las marcas de bola. _____

Translate the following to Spanish:

1. Scare the geese. _____
2. Pick up the geese poop. _____
3. Smile at the members. _____
4. Repair the ball marks. _____
5. Pick up the garbage. _____
6. Cut the holes. _____
7. Rake the bunkers. _____
8. Smile at the players. _____
9. Repair the divots. _____
10. Pick up the flags. _____

ROLE PLAY

Club Championship! It's tournament weekend and you want the course to look awesome for the members and the Greens Committee! Tell your employee to go to (*Vete a*) a hole on the course. Then your partner asks what he should do. Follow the model.

ESTUDIANTE A: Vete a diez . . .
ESTUDIANTE B: ¿Y asusta los gansos?

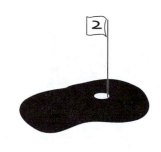   

1.

2.

3.

4.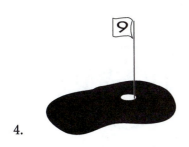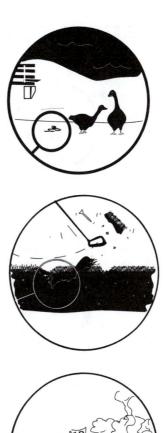

5.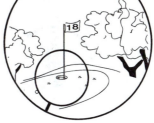

6.

7.

8.

PART II FISHING TERMS

boat
el barco

guide
el guía

fish
el pez

fisherman
el pescador

rod
la caña

reel
el carrete

line
el cordel

bait
la carnada

knot
el nudo

net
la red

camera
la cámara

hat
el sombrero

sunglasses
las gafas de sol

backpack
la mochila

towel
la toalla

MATCHING EXERCISE

Write the letter of the picture next to the Spanish word it matches.

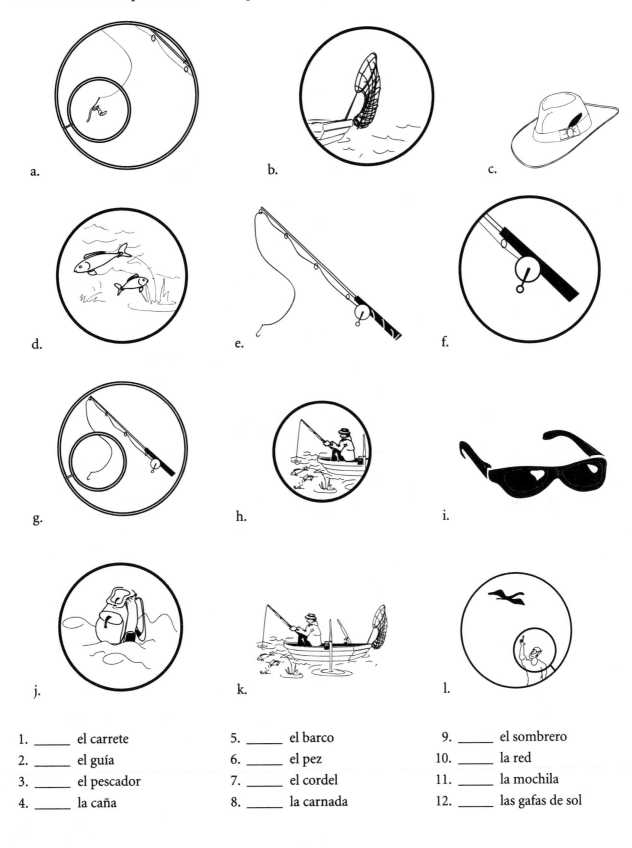

a.

b.

c.

d.

e.

f.

g.

h.

i.

j.

k.

l.

1. _____ el carrete	5. _____ el barco	9. _____ el sombrero
2. _____ el guía	6. _____ el pez	10. _____ la red
3. _____ el pescador	7. _____ el cordel	11. _____ la mochila
4. _____ la caña	8. _____ la carnada	12. _____ las gafas de sol

VOCABULARY EXERCISE

Write the Spanish word for each picture in the space provided.

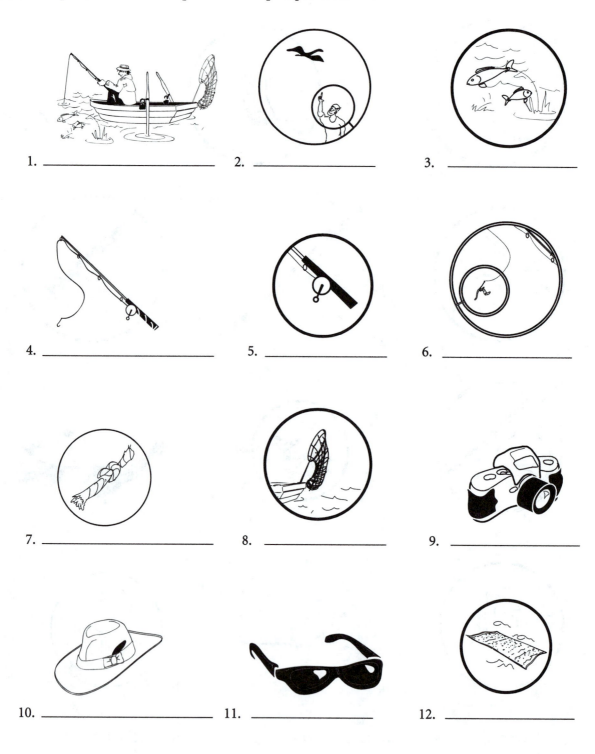

1. _____

2. _____

3. _____

4. _____

5. _____

6. _____

7. _____

8. _____

9. _____

10. _____

11. _____

12. _____

MATCHING EXERCISE

Write the letter of the Spanish word next to the English word it matches on the left.

1. _____ boat
2. _____ guide
3. _____ fish
4. _____ fisherman
5. _____ rod
6. _____ reel
7. _____ line
8. _____ bait

9. _____ knot
10. _____ net
11. _____ camera
12. _____ hat
13. _____ sunglasses
14. _____ backpack
15. _____ towel

a. carnada
b. cordel
c. gafas de sol
d. red
e. mochila
f. caña
g. guía
h. nudo

i. toalla
j. pescador
k. bote
l. pez
m. sombrero
n. carrete
o. cámara

CROSSWORD PUZZLES

Across

3. bait
6. sunglasses
8. camera
11. fisherman
12. boat
13. towel
14. fish

Down

1. rod
2. guide
4. knot
5. line
7. hat
9. net
10. reel

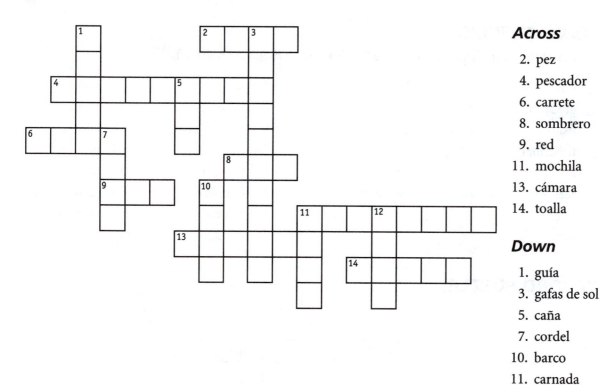

Across

2. pez
4. pescador
6. carrete
8. sombrero
9. red
11. mochila
13. cámara
14. toalla

Down

1. guía
3. gafas de sol
5. caña
7. cordel
10. barco
11. carnada
12. nudo

TRANSLATION EXERCISE

Translate the following to English:

1. el pescador _____
2. la caña _____
3. el cordel _____
4. el barco _____
5. el guía _____
6. el pez _____
7. el sombrero _____
8. la mochila _____
9. las gafas de sol _____
10. la carnada _____
11. el nudo _____
12. la red _____
13. la cámara _____
14. el carrete _____
15. la toalla _____

Translate the following to Spanish:

1. knot _____
2. net _____
3. boat _____
4. guide _____
5. fish _____
6. rod _____
7. reel _____
8. backpack _____
9. towel _____
10. line _____
11. bait _____
12. fisherman _____
13. camera _____
14. hat _____
15. sunglasses _____

MULTIPLE CHOICE

Circle the letter of the correct answer.

1. knot
   a. la red
   b. la caña
   c. el nudo
   d. la mochila

2. net
   a. la caña
   b. el nudo
   c. el bote
   d. la red

3. boat
   a. el bote
   b. el cordel
   c. el red
   d. el pez

4. reel
   a. la caña
   b. el cordel
   c. la carnada
   d. el carrete

5. backpack
   a. la red
   b. la mochila
   c. la carnada
   d. el guía

6. line
   a. el cordel
   b. la red
   c. la carnada
   d. la caña

7. guide
   a. el pescador
   b. el carrete
   c. el guía
   d. el bote

8. fish
   a. la carnada
   b. el pescador
   c. la mochila
   d. el pez

9. rod
   a. la caña
   b. la red
   c. el guía
   d. el nudo

10. bait
   a. las gafas de sol
   b. la carnada
   c. el carrete
   d. el bote

GRAMMAR

To express the word "the" use: *el, la, los, las.*
To express the words "a" and "an" use: *un, una, unas, unos.*

Write the correct form of the words "a", "an", and "some".

1. _____ caña
2. _____ mochilas
3. _____ nudo
4. _____ amigos
5. _____ gafas de sol
6. _____ escoba
7. _____ plantas
8. _____ pico
9. _____ cerveza
10. _____ rastrillos

ROLE PLAY

A. **What do I need?** Pretend you are shopping at your favorite store, Hayes Bait and Tackle Shop. The clerk asks what you need: *¿Qué necesitas?* Respond with: I need *Necesito . . .* Follow the model.

ESTUDIANTE A: ¿Qué necesitas?
ESTUDIANTE B: Necesito un carrete.

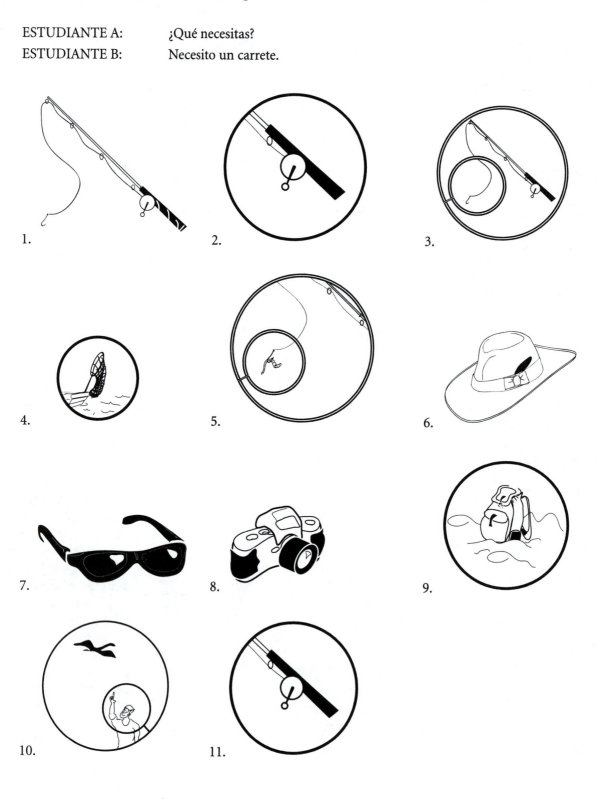

B. **Let's do it all!** You and your friend are planning your trip to Cabo San Lucas, in Baja California. Ask your partner what activities he likes to do on vacation. Use the phrase ¿Te gusta? Tell him you're in agreement by expressing Yes, let's . . . *Sí, vamos a. . .*

ESTUDIANTE A:	¿Te gusta jugar al tenis?
ESTUDIANTE B:	Sí. ¡Vamos a jugar al tenis!

1.

2.

3.

4.

5.

6.

7.

8.

REVIEW

Translate the following to English:

1. Repara las marcas de bola. _____

2. Vete a la área de practica. _____

3. Asusta los gansos. _____

4. Recoge la basura en el campo de golf. _____

5. Necesito una cámara. ¡Sonríe! _____

6. ¿Qué necesitas? _____

7. Necesito un guía y un bote. _____

8. Repara el carrete. _____

9. Corta el cordel. Corta el nudo. _____

10. ¡La red! ¡La red! ¡La cámara! _____

Translate the following to Spanish:

1. Repair the ball marks and the divots. _____

2. Smile at the members and players. _____

3. Scare the geese. _____

4. Pick up the garbage and the goose poop. _____

5. Go to the women's tee. _____

6. Cut the holes. Rake the bunkers. _____

7. What do you need? _____

8. I need a hat and sunglasses. _____

9. I need a rod, reel, line, and bait. _____

10. I need the net and the camera! _____

Read the dialogue aloud with a partner and then translate it to English.

(En la tienda, Live Bait)

Peter: Bienvenidos, Walt! ¿Qué tal?

Walt: ¡Excepcional! Vamos a México el 17 de febrero.

Danny: Sí . . . vamos a pescar. ¿Hay muchos peces en Cabo San Lucas?

Peter: Sí. Y en febrero y marzo hay marlin y tuna. ¿Qué necesitas?

Walt: Necesito una caña y un carrete.

Peter: Ven conmigo, Walt.

Walt: Y cordel . . . mi cordel está en nudos. . .

Peter: (le muestra la manera correcta) Mírame. Hazlo como yo.

Walt: Okay . . . okay. Gracias, Pete.

Peter: Hasta luego.

(en las calles de Cabo San Lucas)

Danny: Primero . . . al hotel.

Walt: No. . .no. ¡Primero al campo de golf!

Danny: No. Primero al banco.

Walt: Buena idea. Eres muy responsable, Dan.

Danny: ¡Y estudio español! Mírame. . .perdón, señora. . .

(Danny habla español con la mujer.)

Mujer: ¿Sí? ¿Qué necesitas?

Danny: Ayúdame, por favor . . . ¿Dónde está el banco?

Mujer: ¿Necesitas un taxi o un guía?

Danny: No, gracias.

Mujer: Está por aquí. . .está cerca. . .

Danny: ¿Está detrás de la iglesia?

Mujer: Sí, está entre las calles Benito Juarez y la Avenida Fox.

Danny: Muchas gracias.

(El Campo de Golf El Dorado)

Walt: Una reservación para dos jugadores, por favor.

Read the dialogue aloud with a partner and then translate it to Spanish.

(In the store, Live Bait)

Peter: Welcome, Walt! How's it going?

Walt: Exceptional! We're going to Mexico on February 17.

Danny: Yes…we're going fishing. Are there many fish in Cabo San Lucas?

Peter: Yes. And in February and March there is marlin and tuna. What do you need?

Walt: I need a rod and reel.

Peter: Come with me, Walt.

Walt: And line…my line is in knots.

Peter: (shows the correct way) Watch me. Do it like me.

Walt: Okay… okay. Thanks, Pete.

Peter: See you later.

(on the streets of Cabo San Lucas)

Danny: First, to the hotel.

Walt: No…no. First to the golf course!

Danny: No. First to the bank.

Walt: Good idea. You're very responsible, Dan.

Danny: And I study Spanish! Watch me…perdón, señora…

(Danny is speaking Spanish with the woman)

Woman: Yes? What do you need?

Danny: Help me, please…Where is the bank?

Woman: Do you need a taxi or a guide?

Danny: No, thank you.

Woman: It's around here…it's near…

Danny: Is it behind the church?

Woman: Yes, it's between Benito Juarez Street and Fox Avenue.

Danny: Thank you.

(El Dorado Golf Course)

Walt: A reservation for two players, please.

Ignacio:	¿Qué día, señor?	**Ignacio:**	What day, sir?
Walt:	El jueves, viernes, y sábado.	**Walt:**	On Thursday, Friday, and Saturday.
Danny:	El sábado, no, Walt. Vamos a pescar el sábado.	**Danny:**	On Saturday, no, Walt. We're going fishing on Saturday.
Walt:	Ah, sí . . . estás muy organizado, Dan.	**Walt:**	Oh, yes…you are very organized, Dan.
Ignacio:	¿A qué hora te gusta jugar el jueves y el viernes?	**Ignacio:**	At what time do you want to play on Thursday and on Friday
Walt:	A las diez, por favor.	**Walt:**	At ten o'clock, please.
(el jueves a las ocho y media)		(on Thursday, 8:30 A.M.)	
Danny:	Buenos días, Walt.	**Danny:**	Good morning, Walt.
Walt:	Aaahhh. . .	**Walt:**	Aaahhh…
Danny:	¿Cómo estás? ¿No estás bien?	**Danny:**	How are you? You're not good?
Walt:	Estoy enfermo. . .	**Walt:**	I'm sick…
Danny:	¿Qué te duele?	**Danny:**	What hurts?
Walt:	Me duele el estómago y la cabeza.	**Walt:**	My stomach and my head hurt.
Danny:	¿Muchas Margaritas, música, y mujeres?	**Danny:**	Many Margaritas, music, and women?
Walt:	Estoy cansado. . .	**Walt:**	I'm tired…
Danny:	¡Vamos! Vamos a comer, Walt.	**Danny:**	Let's go! Let's go eat, Walt.

Translate the following to Spanish:

1. I'm nervous. I'm busy. I'm in a good mood. _____

2. Are you sick or tired? _____

3. The party is Tuesday, October 7. There is pizza and beer. _____

4. What do you like to do? Bowl or play billiards? _____

5. It's bad. Get the first aid kit. _____

6. What hurts? Your eye? Your ear? _____

7. Give me the lawnmower. Mix the oil and gas. _____

8. Where is the gas chainsaw? _____

9. Prune the trees and the shrubs. _____

10. Blow and rake the leaves. _____

11. Load the soil and pine straw. _____

12. Deadhead and fertilize the red annuals. _____

13. Weed the hanging baskets. _____

14. Put the trees in the back yard near the pond. _____

15. Dig a ditch and install the pipe. _____

CULTURE: TIPS FOR THE TRAVELER

Since culture shock is a very real phenomenon, it is important to be well prepared for a foreign trip. Buy and read several travel books about the country to which you are going. The books will tell you the local customs and answer many questions you may have about traveling, tipping, insurance, and so on.

Begin laying out the items you want to bring several days before you actually pack. A few things to remember: your ticket, passport or birth certificate, a money belt or pouch, a dictionary or phrase book, a knife with a bottle opener, your bathing suit, a hat and sunglasses, a camera and film, a novel and a frisbee if you like. Do *not* bring anything illegal across the Mexican border. You will be a happy camper if you pack light!

If you are visiting people, don't forget a small gift from the United States. Some easy-to-carry but much appreciated items are t-shirts with sports logos, baseball caps, and lighters. Be creative.

Practice your new language. Especially with little children.

If you keep a few balloons in your pocket, you can blow them up and it will serve as a way to begin a conversation with them.

It is also important to have in your wallet a list of important numbers. Be sure to make a photocopy of the numbers and leave the copy with a family member or friend. A list of numbers to have include: your birth certificate, passport number, driver's license number, airline tickets, traveler's checks, as well as any credit card numbers.

Before you leave, arrange for the post office to hold your mail until your return. Order foreign currency through your bank for your needs upon arrival ($50.00 to $100.00). Make sure to buy a jug of bottled water before heading to your hotel.

Don't bury yourself in a guidebook. Ask the hotel desk clerks, other hotel staff, or the locals what to do. Get out and explore on your own. Be patient and have fun! Bon voyage!

add	añade	ball	haz bola
adjust	ajusta	ball marks	las marcas de bola
afternoon	tarde	bank	el banco
aggressive	agresivo, a	bark	la corteza
ambitious	ambicioso, a	baseball cap	la gorra
angry	enojado, a	behind	detrás
ankle	el tobillo	between	entre
annuals	las anuales	black	negro
apartments	los apartamentos	blood	la sangre
April	abril	blow	sopla
apply	aplica	blower	la sopladora
Argentinean	argentino (a)	blue	azul
arm	el brazo	boat	el barco
around	alrededor	Bolivian	boliviano (a)
around here	por aquí	boots	las botas
at night	por la noche	boss	el jefe
Attention!	¡Atención!	box	la caja
August	agosto	branches	las ramas
aunt	la tía	bricks	los ladrillos
bad mood	de mal humor	bring	trae
back	la espalda	broom	la escoba
backpack	la mochila	brother	el hermano
back yard	el jardín de atrás	brown	café
bait	la carnada	brush	cepilla
bag	el saco	bunker	la trampa

building	el edificio	day	el día
Burns!	¡Quema!	daughter	la hija
burlap	pon en costal	deadhead	corta la mala
busy	ocupado, a	December	diciembre
camera	la cámara	dig	excava
can	la lata	dig up	saca
car trunk	el baúl	divots	las raspadas
cart	el carrito	dog	el perro
cement	el cemento	Dominican	dominicano (a)
cemetery	el cementerio	down, below	abajo
check	checa	driveway	la calzada
chest	el pecho	driving range	la área de práctica
children	los hijos	ear	el oído
Chilean	chileno (a)	earplugs	los tapones para los oídos
church	la iglesia		
clay	el barro	early	temprano
clean	limpia	east	este
clippings	el cortado	Ecuadorian	ecuatoriano (a)
close	cerca	elbow	el codo
comical	cómico, a	exactly, sharp	en punto
compost	el abono	Excellent!	¡Excelente!
confused	confundido, a	Exceptional!	¡Excepcional!
connect	conecta	extroverted	extrovertido, a
container	el recipiente	eye	el ojo
content	contento, a	Fabulous!	¡Fabuloso!
cooperative	cooperativo, a	fair	justo, a
Costa Rican	costarricense	fall	el otoño
cousin	el (la) primo(a)	family	la familia
crew	la cuadrilla	Fantastic!	¡Fantástico!
cruel	cruel	far	lejos
Cuban	cubano (a)	father	el padre
customer	el (la) cliente	February	febrero
cut	corta	feet	los pies
Danger!	¡Peligro!	fence	la cerca

fertilizer	**el fertilizante**	green	**verde**
fingers	**los dedos**	grey	**gris**
fire extinguisher	**el extinguidor**	Guatemalan	**guatemalteco (a)**
first	**primero**	guide	**el guía**
first aid kit	**el botiquín**	happy	**feliz**
fish	**el pez**	hardworking	**trabajador / trabajadora**
fisherman	**el pescador**		
flags	**las banderas**	hand	**la mano**
flat	**el flat**	hanging baskets	**las canastas colgadas**
flowers	**las flores**	hat	**el sombrero**
flush	**saca el agua**	head	**la cabeza**
foreman, crew leader	**el mayordomo**	here	**aquí**
fountain	**la fuente**	hi/hello	**hola**
Friday	**viernes**	hold	**agarra**
friends	**los amigos**	hole, cup	**el hoyo, la copa**
front yard	**el jardín de enfrente**	Honduran	**hondureño (a)**
furious	**furioso, a**	honest	**honesto, a**
gallons	**los galones**	hose	**la manguera**
garage	**el garaje**	hospital	**el hospital**
garbage	**la basura**	Hot!	**¡Caliente!**
gas	**la gasolina**	hotel	**el hotel**
gas chainsaw	**el serrucho de gas**	house	**la casa**
gate	**la puerta**	how	**cómo**
geese	**los gansos**	husband	**el esposo**
geese poop	**la mierda de los gansos**	I am. . .	**Estoy. . .**
		I'm . . .	**Soy . . .**
generous	**generoso, a**	impatient	**impaciente**
get	**consigue**	impulsive	**impulsivo, a**
gloves	**los guantes**	inches	**las pulgadas**
golf cart	**el carrito**	in the afternoon	**por la tarde**
golf course	**el campo de golf**	in the morning	**por la mañana**
goodbye	**Adiós**	independent	**independiente**
grandparents	**los abuelos**	in front	**delante**
grass	**el zacate, el pasto**	in, on	**en**

inside	**dentro**	mother	**la madre**
install	**instala**	move	**mueve**
intellectual	**intelectual**	mulch	**muele**
intelligent	**inteligente**	mulch (mixture)	**la mezcla**
introverted	**introvertido, a**	names	**los nombres**
January	**enero**	near	**cerca**
June	**junio**	neck	**el cuello**
July	**julio**	neighbor	**el vecino**
knee	**la rodilla**	net	**la red**
knot	**el nudo**	nervious	**nervioso, a**
late	**tarde**	Nicaraguan	**nicaragüense**
lawnmower	**la máquina**	night	**noche**
leaf rake	**el rastrillo de hojas**	north	**norte**
leak	**la fuga**	November	**noviembre**
leaves	**las hojas**	nozzle	**la boquilla**
left	**izquierda**	October	**octubre**
leg	**la pierna**	oil	**el aceite**
library	**la biblioteca**	on time	**a tiempo**
line	**el cordel**	on top	**encima**
load	**carga**	only	**solamente**
Magnificent!	**¡Magnífico!**	open	**abre**
man	**el hombre**	over	**sobre**
manager	**el (la) gerente**	over there	**allá**
March	**marzo**	orange	**anaranjado**
Marvelous!	**¡Maravilloso!**	organized	**organizado, a**
materialistic	**materialisto, a**	outside	**fuera**
May	**mayo**	pack	**empaca**
members	**los miembros**	pallet	**la paleta**
men's tee	**el tee de hombres**	Panamanian	**panameño (a)**
Mexican	**mexicano (a)**	Paraguayan	**paraguayo (a)**
mix	**mezcla**	parents	**los padres**
Monday	**lunes**	park	**el parque**
month	**el mes**	parking lot	**el aparcamiento**
morning	**mañana**	path	**el sendero**

patient	**paciente**
patio	**el patio**
peat moss	**la turba**
perennials	**las perennes**
Perfect!	**¡Perfecto!**
Peruvian	**peruano (a)**
pick	**el pico**
pick up	**recoge**
pile	**el montón**
pine straw	**la paja**
pink	**rosado**
pipe	**la pipa**
pitchfork	**la horca**
play, to	**jugar**
players	**los jugadores**
plant	**planta**
plants	**las plantas**
please	**por favor**
pond	**el estanque**
pool	**la alberca**
pot (plastic, clay)	**la maceta (de plástico, de barro)**
pot	**la maceta**
pot, to	**planta**
potting bench	**la mesa de plantar**
prepare	**prepara**
prices	**los precios**
prune	**poda**
pruner	**la podadera**
Puerto Rican	**puertorriqueño (a)**
pull	**jala**
purple	**morado**
push	**empuja**
push broom	**el cepillo**

put away	**guarda**
put, tag	**pon**
rake	**el rastrillo**
red	**rojo**
reel	**el carrete**
repair	**repara**
replace	**reemplaza**
repot	**replanta**
responsible	**responsable**
restaurant	**el restaurante**
return	**regresa**
right	**derecha**
rock	**la roca**
rod	**la caña**
romantic	**romántico, a**
roots	**las raíces**
rototiller	**el rototiller**
sad	**triste**
safety helmet	**el casco de seguridad**
safety glasses	**los lentes de seguridad**
Salvadorian	**salvadoreño (a)**
sand	**la arena**
Saturday	**sábado**
scare	**asusta**
school	**la escuela**
second	**segundo**
secretary	**la secretaria**
seeds	**las semillas**
sensitive	**sencible**
September	**septiembre**
shade	**la sombra**
shopping mall	**el mall**
shoulder	**el hombro**

shovel	la pala	third	tercero
shrubs	los arbustos	Thursday	jueves
sick	enfermo, a	timid	tímido, a
sidewalk	la banqueta	tired	cansado, a
sincere	sincero, a	tires	las llantas
sister	la hermana	today	hoy
sledgehammer	el marro, el mazo	tomorrow	mañana
smile	sonríe	tomorrow afternoon	mañana por la tarde
sociable	sociable	tomorrow morning	mañana por la mañana
sod	el zacate		
soil	la tierra	tomorrow night	mañana por la noche
soil rake	el rastrillo de tierra	towel	la toalla
son	el hijo	trees	los árboles
south	sur	trench	la zanja
spray	rocia	Tuesday	martes
spread	empareja	uncle	el tío
spring	la primavera	uniform	el uniforme
sprinkler	el rociador	United States	estadounidense
sprinkler heads	las cabezas	unload	descarga
stomach	el estómogo	university	la universidad
stones	las piedras	up, above	arriba
store	la tienda	Uruguayan	uruguayo (a)
street	la calle	use	usa
summer	el verano	valve	la válvula
sun	el sol	Venezuelan	venezolano (a)
sunglasses	las gafas de sol	Warning!	¡Aviso!
Sunday	domingo	wash	lava
superstitious	supersticioso, a	water	el agua
sweep	barre	watering	riega
tags, labels	las etiquetas	Wednesday	miércoles
take out	saca	weed, to	desherbar
technician	el mecánico	weeds	las hierbas
thank you	gracias	week	la semana
there	allí	weekend	el fin de semana

welcome	**bienvenidos**	wife	**la esposa**
west	**oeste**	winter	**el invierno**
what	**qué**	wire	**el alambre**
wheelbarrow	**la carretilla**	woman	**la mujer**
where	**dónde**	women's tee	**el tee de mujeres**
where is	**dónde está**	worried	**preocupado, a**
when	**cuándo**	wrap	**envuelve**
white	**blanco**	yards	**las yardas**
who	**quién**	year	**el año**
who, what, where	**quién, qué, dónde**	yellow	**amarillo**
why	**por qué**	yesterday	**ayer**

abajo	**down, below**	amarillo	**yellow**
el abono	**compost**	aquí	**here**
abre	**open**	los árboles	**trees**
abril	**April**	los arbustos	**shrubs**
los abuelos	**grandparents**	la área de práctica	**driving range**
el aceite	**oil**	la arena	**sand**
adiós	**goodbye**	argentino (a)	**Argentinean**
agarra	**hold**	arriba	**up, above**
agosto	**August**	asusta	**scare**
agresivo, a	**aggressive**	¡Atención!	**Attention!**
el agua	**water**	¡Aviso!	**Warning!**
ajusta	**adjust**	ayer	**yesterday**
el alambre	**wire**	azul	**blue**
la alberca	**pool**	el banco	**bank**
allá	**over there**	las banderas	**flags**
allí	**there**	la banqueta	**sidewalk**
alrededor	**around**	el barco	**boat**
ambicioso, a	**ambitious**	barre	**sweep**
los amigos	**friends**	el barro	**clay**
añade	**add**	la basura	**garbage**
anaranjado	**orange**	la biblioteca	**library**
el año	**year**	bienvenidos	**welcome**
las anuales	**annuals**	blanco	**white**
el aparcamiento	**parking lot**	boliviano (a)	**Bolivian**
los apartamentos	**apartments**	la boquilla	**nozzle**
aplica	**apply**	las botas	**boots**

el botiquín	**first aid kit**	conecta	**connect**
el brazo	**arm**	confundido, a	**confused**
la cabeza	**head**	consigue	**get**
las cabezas	**sprinkler heads**	cooperativo, a	**cooperative**
café	**brown**	contento, a	**content**
la caja	**box**	el cordel	**line**
¡Caliente!	**Hot!**	corta	**cut**
la calle	**street**	corta la mala	**deadhead**
la calzada	**driveway**	el cortado	**clippings**
la cámara	**camera**	la corteza	**bark**
el campo de golf	**golf course**	pon en costal	**burlap**
la caña	**rod**	cruel	**cruel**
cansado, a	**tired**	la cuadrilla	**crew**
las canastas colgadas	**hanging baskets**	cuándo	**when**
carga	**load**	cubano (a)	**Cuban**
la carnada	**bait**	el cuello	**neck**
la carretilla	**wheelbarrow**	dentro	**inside**
el carrete	**reel**	derecha	**right**
el carrito	**cart**	detrás	**behind**
la casa	**house**	descarga	**unload**
el casco de seguridad	**safety helmet**	desherbar	**weed, to**
el cemento	**cement**	el día	**day**
el cementerio	**cemetery**	diciembre	**December**
la cepilla	**brush**	domingo	**Sunday**
el cepillo	**push broom**	dominicano (a)	**Dominican**
cerca	**near**	dónde	**where**
la cerca	**fence**	los dedos	**fingers**
checa	**check**	ecuatoriano (a)	**Ecuadorian**
chileno (a)	**Chilean**	el edificio	**building**
cierra	**close**	empaca	**pack**
el cliente	**customer**	empuja	**push**
el codo	**elbow**	en	**in, on**
cómico, a	**comical**	encima	**on top**
cómo	**how**	enero	**January**

enfermo, a	**sick**	furioso, a	**furious**
en punto	**exactly, sharp**	las gafas de sol	**sunglasses**
enojado, a	**angry**	los galones	**gallons**
entre	**between**	los gansos	**geese**
envuelve	**wrap**	el garaje	**garage**
empareja	**spread**	la gasolina	**gas**
la escoba	**broom**	generoso, a	**generous**
la escuela	**school**	el (la) gerente	**manager**
la espalda	**back**	gracias	**thank you**
la esposa	**wife**	gris	**grey**
el esposo	**husband**	los guantes	**gloves**
estadounidense	**United States**	guarda	**put away**
el estanque	**pond**	guatemalteco (a)	**Guatemalan**
este	**east**	el guía	**guide**
el estómogo	**stomach**	haz bola	**ball**
las etiquetas	**tags, labels**	las hierbas	**weeds**
excava	**dig**	la hija	**daughter**
¡Excelente!	**Excellent!**	el hijo	**son**
¡Excepcional!	**Exceptional!**	los hijos	**children**
el extinguidor	**fire extinguisher**	la hermana	**sister**
extrovertido, a	**extroverted**	el hermano	**brother**
¡Fabuloso!	**Fabulous!**	las hojas	**leaves**
la familia	**family**	hola	**hi/hello**
¡Fantástico!	**Fantastic!**	hondureño (a)	**Honduran**
por favor	**please**	honesto, a	**honest**
el fertilizante	**fertilizer**	el hombre	**man**
febrero	**February**	el hombro	**shoulder**
feliz	**happy**	la horca	**pitchfork**
el fin de semana	**weekend**	el hospital	**hospital**
el flat	**flat**	el hotel	**hotel**
las flores	**flowers**	hoy	**today**
la fuente	**fountain**	el hoyo	**hole**
fuera	**outside**	el hoyo, la copa	**hole, cup**
la fuga	**leak**	la iglesia	**church**

impaciente	impatient	mañana por la noche	tomorrow night
impulsivo, a	impulsive	la manguera	hose
independiente	independent	la mano	hand
instala	install	la máquina	lawnmower
intelectual	intellectual	¡Maravilloso!	Marvelous!
inteligente	intelligent	el marro, el mazo	sledgehammer
introvertido, a	introverted	martes	Tuesday
el invierno	winter	marzo	March
izquierda	left	materialisto, a	materialistic
jala	pull	mayo	May
el jardín de atrás	back yard	el mayordomo	foreman, crew leader
el jardín de enfrente	front yard	el mecánico	technician
el jefe	boss	mexicano (a)	Mexican
jueves	Thursday	el mes	month
los jugadores	players	la mesa de plantar	potting bench
julio	July	mezcla	mix
junio	June	la mezcla	mulch (mixture)
justo, a	fair	miércoles	Wednesday
lava	wash	los miembros	members
lejos	far	la mierda de los gansos	geese poop
los ladrillos	bricks	la mochila	backpack
la lata	can	el montón	pile
las llantas	tires	morado	purple
los lentes de seguridad	safety glasses	mueve	move
limpia	clean	muele	mulch
lunes	Monday	la mujer	woman
el mall	shopping mall	negro	black
la maceta	pot	nervioso, a	nervious
la madre	mother	nicaragüense	Nicaraguan
¡Magnífico!	Magnificent!	noche	night
mañana	tomorrow	los nombres	names
mañana	morning	norte	north
mañana por la tarde	tomorrow afternoon	noviembre	November
mañana por la mañana	tomorrow morning	el nudo	knot

ocupado, a	**busy**	poda	**prune**
octubre	**October**	la podadera	**pruner**
oeste	**west**	pon	**put, tag**
el oído	**ear**	pon en costal	**burlap**
el ojo	**eye**	por qué	**why**
organizado, a	**organized**	preocupado, a	**worried**
el otoño	**fall**	los precios	**prices**
paciente	**patient**	prepara	**prepare**
el padre	**father**	la primavera	**spring**
los padres	**parents**	primero	**first**
la paleta	**pallet**	el (la) primo(a)	**cousin**
panameño (a)	**Panamanian**	la puerta	**gate**
la paja	**pine straw**	puertorriqueño (a)	**Puerto Rican**
la pala	**shovel**	las pulgadas	**inches**
paraguayo (a)	**Paraguayan**	qué	**what**
el parque	**park**	¡Quema!	**Burns!**
el patio	**patio**	quién	**who**
el pecho	**chest**	las raíces	**roots**
¡Peligro!	**Danger!**	las ramas	**branches**
¡Perfecto!	**Perfect!**	las raspadas	**divots**
las perennes	**perennials**	el rastrillo	**rake**
el perro	**dog**	el rastrillo de tierra	**soil rake**
peruano (a)	**Peruvian**	el rastrillo de hojas	**leaf rake**
el pescador	**fisherman**	el recipiente	**container**
el pez	**fish**	riega	**water**
el pico	**pick**	recoge	**pick up**
las piedras	**stones**	la red	**net**
la pierna	**leg**	reemplaza	**replace**
los pies	**feet**	regresa	**return**
la pipa	**pipe**	repara	**repair**
planta	**plant**	replanta	**repot**
planta	**pot , to**	responsable	**responsible**
las plantas	**plants**	el restaurante	**restaurant**
la plastalina	**clay**	la roca	**rock**

rocia	**spray**	los tapones para los oídos	**earplugs**
el rociador	**sprinkler**	tarde	**afternoon**
la rodilla	**knee**	tarde	**late**
rojo	**red**	temprano	**early**
romántico, a	**romantic**	el tee de hombres	**men's tee**
rosado	**pink**	el tee de mujeres	**women's tee**
el rototiller	**rototiller**	tercero	**third**
sábado	**Saturday**	la tía	**aunt**
saca	**take out**	a tiempo	**on time**
saca el agua	**flush**	la tienda	**store**
el saco	**bag**	la tierra	**soil**
la sangre	**blood**	tímido, a	**timid**
salvadoreño (a)	**Salvadorian**	el tío	**uncle**
segundo	**second**	la toalla	**towel**
la secretaria	**secretary**	el tobillo	**ankle**
la semana	**week**	trabajador / trabajadora	**hardworking**
las semillas	**seeds**	trae	**bring**
sencible	**sensitive**	la trampa	**bunker**
el sendero	**path**	triste	**sad**
septiembre	**September**	la turba	**peat moss**
el serrucho de gas	**gas chainsaw**	el uniforme	**uniform**
sincero, a	**sincere**	la universidad	**university**
sobre	**over**	uruguayo (a)	**Uruguayan**
sociable	**sociable**	usa	**use**
el sol	**sun**	la válvula	**valve**
solamente	**only**	el vecino	**neighbor**
sonríe	**smile**	viernes	**Friday**
la sombra	**shade**	venezolano (a)	**Venezuelan**
el sombrero	**hat**	el verano	**summer**
sopla	**blow**	verde	**green**
la sopladora	**blower**	las yardas	**yards**
Soy . . .	**I'm . . .**	el zacate, el pasto	**grass**
supersticioso, a	**superstitious**	el zacate	**sod**
sur	**south**	la zanja	**trench**